Theologians in Transition

THEOLOGIANS IN TRANSITION

The Christian Century
"How My Mind Has Changed" Series

Edited by JAMES M. WALL

With an Introduction by
MARTIN E. MARTY

CROSSROAD · NEW YORK

1981
The Crossroad Publishing Company
575 Lexington Avenue, New York, NY 10022

Printed in the United States of America

Library of Congress Cataloging in Publication Data

Main entry under title:
Theologians in transition.

   Twenty-one essays originally published in The Christian
century in 1980 and 1981.
   1. Theology—20th century—Addresses, essays, lectures.
2. Theologians—Addresses, essays, lectures. I. Wall,
James McKendree, 1928-   II. Christian century.
BR50.T42158   230'.09'04   81-9875
ISBN 0-8245-0101-2   AACR2
ISBN 0-8245-0103-9 (pbk.)

To HAROLD E. FEY,
Christian Century Editor from 1956 to 1964

Contents

Acknowledgments

This book is the product of the ideas and efforts of many persons. Thanks are due first of all to the twenty-one theologians who wrote these essays, which appeared originally in *The Christian Century* during 1980 and 1981 in the magazine's "How My Mind Has Changed" series. I am grateful for their willingness to share their theological turns and transitions with readers. I am likewise grateful to the entire staff of *The Christian Century* for their contributions: in particular, to associate editor Martin E. Marty, who played a major role in the selection of authors and wrote the introduction; to associate editor Jean Caffey Lyles, who edited the manuscripts and did the final proofreading; to associate editor Linda Marie Delloff, who coordinated arrangements between the *Century* offices and the Crossroad Publishing Company; to managing editor Dean Peerman, who made many helpful suggestions and corrections with an eye for accuracy and precision; to Elaine Kreis, Sydell Reeves, and Kathleen Wind, who typed the manuscripts; and to Barbara Nelson Gingerich and Karen Summers, who assisted with proofreading.

Finally, this book is dedicated to Harold E. Fey, who served, from 1956 to 1964, as the third of six *Christian Century* editors. Harold, who is still on the *Century* masthead as a contributing editor, was involved in continuing the tradition of once-a-decade presentation of how theological thinking has changed. He remains a strong supporter and counselor to editors who are grateful that he continues, in semiretirement, to inspire and counsel his successors.

James M. Wall

Theologians in Transition

Introduction

MARTIN E. MARTY
How Their Minds Have Changed

Their enemies would call every author in this book (but one) a theological liberal. Whatever their own chosen nuances, most of them would be ready to live with such a label, unfashionable as it may sound. Liberals, according to conventional wisdom, read the signs of the times, adapt to them, and make Christian theology come out right. Thus they gain the favor of the culture, stimulate a market for their writings and a clientele for their preachments, and succumb to the *Zeitgeist*.

To be in step today, as any market analyst could tell after five minutes with opinion polls and growth graphs, would imply two basic decisions—one theological or ecclesiastical and one political. Ecclesiastically, in the face of almost overwhelming pluralism, leaders should help their people withdraw from positive contact with others. They should build walls around their own gatherings, give negative images of outsiders, preach absolutism, insist on authority to back their viewpoints, and be aggressive about keeping all but converts at a distance. Secondly, in a time of political conservatism, retreat from pacific gestures into militancy, and rejection of other peoples' ideologies, they should use their religious outlook to justify their own national political and economic systems. Then they will prosper—and liberals want to prosper.

To be in step, then, the market analyst would have to tell almost all the authors in this book that they are wrong. *Out of step.* Walking or running or swimming against the slope and the wind and the tide. In the first case, instead of withdrawing into constrictive circles, they all call for a more urgent encounter with world religions and with individual religiosities of alien and often uncongenial stripe—in the name of Jesus Christ and the God of the Christian faith. And politically, the second half of the book is given over to authors who say, contrary to the opinion polls, that Christian theology should be rooted not only in the tradition of dominant Euro-Americans of privileged class and gender. Believers can be faithful to the Christian message by being responsive to the strivings of people who have not shared the tradition or the privilege.

If being in step is what liberalism is about, then some liberals are these! They are either misreading the times or selling out the tradition. Who are they, and why are they speaking up? We owe readers an explanation. The chapters in this book grew out of a magazine series, and I have been invited, as an editor of the magazine, first to take the reader behind the scenes and then to anticipate the argument of these two companies of theologians and writers.

On January 18, 1939, contributors to *The Christian Century* began to make theological history by telling readers how their minds had changed. Since the period on which they were to report was a decade, the 1979–80 sequence of the "How My Mind Has Changed" series makes possible an assessment of exactly a half-century of change in religious thought. No one living recalls what decisions went into the invention of the first series or what debates followed concerning the selection of authors.

Some of us remember the editors who were involved at the time (and their consultants) and know that they were as contentious and opinionated as their successors. So they must have generated a good deal of ruckus on Chicago's South Dearborn Street. But from that first series and the follow-ups that help make up an astonishing evidence of continuity in religious journalism came, by ripple effect, a recurrent secondary debate that did much to shape subsequent theology.

The very notion of a set of articles on how theologians had changed their minds provoked criticism from the beginning. The standard charge at first came from static scholastic thinkers: theology was simply the truth, or no one should voice it at all. If one knew the truth, to admit a change of mind had to mean a loss or even a denial of truth. To portray religious thinkers as fickle enough to be able to detect shifts in their own outlooks within a span as short as ten years might introduce a sense of relativism or certainly of shakiness to an enterprise that demanded confidence from those who were its clientele.

That type of criticism has diminished with the passing of the decades. Roman Catholicism admits to having changed. In fact, at the Second Vatican Council the highest authorities of the church recognized development, revision and re-revisioning of doctrine itself in formal documents like the Declaration on Religious Freedom. While the more rock-ribbed fundamentalists may still insist that we must agree to disagree—we doing things our way and they, changelessly, doing things God's way—moderate evangelicals relish talk about their own development. John Henry Newman seems to be winning the day: to change is to grow, and to have changed often is to have grown much. (Some reservations might be sounded about the outer reaches of what that statement implies, but the first half seems valid enough.)

The second area of controversy has issued not so much from the majority of readers—who have found this medium to be the most palatable form of theological discourse they know. Instead, the complainants are some of the writers and a small group among the readers. They find that the articles in the series are too carefully noted, too well remembered. Paul Tillich, whose copy received the blue-pencil treatment from our copy editor, told me that his article in the series brought forth more admiration than any other piece of his he could recollect. People especially liked its style. I asked him how *he* accounted for the clarity. Oblivious of the fact that his Angloteutonism had been Englished in our office, he answered, "Oh, that's easy: I wrote it at A-ca-*pul*-co."

Tillich loved an audience and did not seem to mind being a bit unbuttoned and informal in this personal mode. But other theologians are trained to be ultraspecialists, to cultivate an academic style that alienates all but fellow insiders. Some follow this path out of fear of unsheltered life beyond the academy, some as part of the ivory-tower mystique, but most, let us assume (some of my best friends are theologians), do so in order to protect the integrity of thought and language. As part of their career-long search for a voice, many of them expunge the first-person-singular pronoun from their vocabulary and blush to introduce it here where they must. Some have tried circumlocutions like "the present writer," but these translate simply to "I." The genre impels theologians to say not only what they think but why they think it. And the "why" does not always find its way into their formal articles. The pieces they write for this series tend to be, well, interesting.

When the first series came out, I was not yet reading theology; *Moby Dick* and *Treasure Island* were my standard literary fare. My first encounter with the discipline came at seminary when I was reading *about The Christian Century*, not reading *The Christian Century*. During the present season of reminiscence it seems worthwhile to revisit the *History of Chris-*

tian Thought, whose second volume concluded with reference to the *Century's* "startling series" of 1939. History authors J. L. Neve and O. W. Heick were moderately conservative Lutherans who had no special truck with the generally liberal writers corralled by editor Charles Clayton Morrison and company. But they reported fairly and with proper instincts concerning the significance of main themes about the turnings of the decade. Morrison, by the way, chose 34 contributors, which made his work easier than is ours in a more selective day; John C. Bennett and E. G. Homrighausen from that all-but-Barth-being-American cast still write for us, but the others were older when first asked, or have been lost to us for various reasons.

Frankly, none of the later decades saw such a decisive turn on a single issue as did the one portrayed by the writers of 1939. We can here quote a few Neve-Heickian excerpts to show how almost all contributors to that series wrestled with liberalism itself after the period in which imported European neo-orthodoxy fused with native-grown Christian realism à la the Niebuhr brothers. The optimism which World War I had by 1919 destroyed on the Continent lived on until the Depression in America; around 1933 there seemed to be a sense of challenge for everyone to change minds. Morrison: "A whole new theological outlook had emerged. The liberalism which had been for nearly a half-century the common presupposition of Christian scholarship had been for the first time effectively challenged." Some liberals like Robert L. Calhoun were "bandaged but unbowed," and Bennett allowed that his "natural Pelagianism" was only slightly qualified in that period of time. Some doughty fighters like Edgar S. Brightman viewed with regret "the rising tide of neosupernaturalism and Barthianism." Karl Barth enjoyed the rising tide of neosupernaturalism and Barthianism.

Along with Barth, the other lion among the series contributors was Reinhold Niebuhr, who had done plenty of mind-changing in the 1930s: "I underwent a fairly complete conversion of thought which involved rejection of almost all the liberal theological ideals and ideas with which I ventured forth in 1915." Niebuhr no longer had faith in human capacity to subdue nature, or faith that the subjection of nature achieves life's final good. "Faith in man's essential goodness" also suffered. His were themes congenial to Karl Barth, who so enjoyed being asked about his mind-changing that he collected his Niebuhr-record-tying three contributions into a book with the more assertive title, *How I Changed My Mind* (John Knox, 1966). Some find the collection to be the best chronology or autobiography of his mental journey. Barth set the proper tone in the first line of the first essay:

> The editor of *The Christian Century* is insistent that the contributions on this theme should be made as personal and "autobiographical" as possible. And why should I not comply with this wish? Have I not often enough exerted myself to write in a scholarly, systematically precise manner—and also edifyingly, arousingly, polemically? Why not then also for once "autobiographically"?

The collection at the end of the 1950s included a broader spectrum than Morrison's mainline-to-left of Protestantism. Five contributors are still active: Bennett, Albert Outler, Billy Graham, L. Harold deWolf, and the somewhat younger William Hordern. Along the way we lost Karl Barth, Martin Luther King, Jr., H. Richard and Reinhold Niebuhr, Edward John Carnell, Will Herberg, Paul Tillich and James Pike from that select list of 13 worthy mind-changers of the '50s. Some innovations were apparent by 1959. The names of Carnell and Graham signaled a recognition of the more vocal evangelical camp, and Herberg was a Jew, though not the first in these series. There were not as yet any Roman Catholics or Eastern Orthodox, and only one woman, Georgia Harkness, had broken the ranks. Editor Harold E. Fey found among the consistent strands in this collection a preoccupation with the churches at home and the cold war abroad. He also detected signs of "the revolution of rising expectations," but could not yet surmise what this might mean for the churches. Then came the '60s, when those expectations became vivid in the tumult of racial change, feminism, the new ethnicity, the generation gap and a fresh consciousness of the Third World.

Changes over the most recent decade are of special interest to us, so a page-through with reference to the series of 1969–70 should be rewarding. Bishop John A. T. Robinson kicked off by suggesting that he was never so conservative before *Honest to God*, nor so radical after, as many had thought; the subsequent decade has found him snuggling back to his roots in biblical scholarship. Dom Helder Câmara has followed the trajectory he then outlined after his conversion from staidness to a Christian position of demand for radical social change. Reinhold Niebuhr appeared for a third time to signal his intensified interest in Protestant-Catholic encounter.

Robert McAfee Brown did not at that time lay forth the preoccupation with liberation theology that has engrossed him in the '70s, but the tilt was there, and he was taking pains not to let his political instinct lead him to drift toward humanism. Jacques Ellul was as uncompromising in his judgmental note about church and society as he would have been a decade earlier and is now. His mind-change led him toward political withdrawal and ever more radical thought, he thought. Jürgen Moltmann was on the course he has followed with his political theology of hope. Harvey Cox interviewed himself in order to dwell not on the substance of his thought but on the process of changing. Emil J. Fackenheim was on the way to firming up the approach that has come to dominate his work: Jews are now forbidden to take any actions that might make a new Hitler possible. Sidney E. Mead spoke up then, as he has ever more stridently in the ensuing years, for "the religion of the republic" and against sectarianism of the sects.

In his article for the series, John L. McKenzie, a Roman Catholic biblical scholar, showed how free Catholicism was to be absorbed into historical contexts and also showed how McKenzie-ish he was by concluding, "The Christian church has not yet proclaimed the whole gospel"; McKenzie still prods it to do such proclaiming. J. M. Lochman wrote about radical secularity and radical grace from a middle-European Protestant point of view, as he still does. Cynthia Wedel, the second woman in the total series, urged the churches to find new modes to relate to social action, viewing the successful models of the '60s as now in need of replacement. In our midwestern province we have heard less frequently from an Eastern Orthodox representative; Paul Verghese, a Syrian Orthodox priest from Kerala, India (who has since become Bishop Paulos Gregorios), plumped for a sacramental humanism. And William Stringfellow closed the book on the decade with a trumpet blast in a minor key against churches for their compromise of social justice even as he spoke of his "second birthday," having outlasted a terrible disease. The Stringfellow theme has also been consistent through the decade. One happy note: all but one of this group, Reinhold Niebuhr, are around to read how their successors are thinking about thinking in the religious context today.

In this book there seem to be two sets of minds undergoing two types of changes. Another way to put it is that the reader is getting two books for the price of one. Of course there is significant overlap between the two themes and the ways writers treat them. But much of the time they also seem to be on parallel tracks.

The second half derives more from the revolutions of Christian consciousness that occurred in the 1960s and live on now under the code name "liberation theology." The first half reacts more to the changes that became visible during the '70s, and concentrates on two basic shifts: from the secular to the religious paradigm, and from the provincial reading of exclusive Christianity to the problem of pluralism and a renewed interest in universalism.

The writers in the second half for the most part have undergone less mind-changing, except that, with the revolutions partly spent in North America, they seem to come across more gently and with less sense of being on a winning side. The writers in the first half, with only a couple of exceptions, underwent more experience of change. Let us talk about them and their vision first.

Fundamental to all but one of the essays in the first half has been the shift to which Peter Berger and Langdon Gilkey refer in theme-setting opening chapters. In the 1960s most of them had observed or even bought into a model of theology that had been taking shape for four centuries. The pagan themes in the Renaissance had shown that there was already then some wavering in support of the Christian world view. The Promethean mood of artists and scientists, political figures and inventors set a style that has endured despite occasional reactions. The theologians of the 1960s also inherited much from the Enlightenment: a belief in reason, science, politics and human achievement. On the negative side, the Enlightened had opposed "superstition and priestcraft," and the theologians of the '60s joined in interpreting the signs of their times as one in which magic, mystery, metaphysics, myth and mysticism were forever fading from human history—at least from its advance guard, the technological and well-educated West. Nor would the church count for much after this final unfolding of the Industrial Revolution had worked its effects.

To the Renaissance-Enlightenment mood of confidence these theologians of "the secular city," when being "honest to God," saw God, the divine, the sacred and religiosity to be problematic. From the 19th century they borrowed the cultural and sometimes theological critiques of God-talk and God-experience. Nietzsche, Darwin, Marx and, from the 20th century, Freud as God-killers spoke to their situation. And from the 20th century they picked up two sets of motifs. One was neo-orthodoxy's criticism of religion, about which more later. The other was a theology that derived from people like Friedrich Gogarten and Dietrich Bonhoeffer. Both of them were tired of the disgraceful retreat by Christians in the face of every new human unfolding, whether in science or humanism. So they projected what Bonhoeffer called a "religionless Christianity." The new theologians read Christian theology as Gogarten did, and saw it as a working out of biblical critiques of religion. The Bible had, all along, as a main motif the idea that Yahweh or the Father of Jesus Christ would do away with imprisoning myths and religious preoccupations. God would be served as much in the marketplace as in the sanctuary, in the streets as in the monasteries. They foresaw a world of rather sunny agnostics who might somehow be moved by a few retrieved liberating themes from the Christian story and symbolic pool.

There were some good reasons for reading human history on this trajectory, but these were developed in no small measure from the provincial context in which theology was being written. For the most part, it had become a university discipline that occasionally reached out into the worlds of politics and the media. More and more it was divorced from the life of the churches, where in day-to-day existence people asked the timeless questions of meaning and belonging, of religion and church. Now it happened that the academy was perhaps the only place where "secular man," as he or she was then known, was dominating. The theologians in a sense asked how they could become relevant to their fellows who seldom asked metaphysical questions or exposed to view their own struggles with meaning. Politics and mass media of communications drew people who were aware of the problems of religious pluralism, in which setting one wishes to offend no groups and settles for being silent about religion. The theologians who dealt with leaders in these spheres or who took their cultural reading from these people also saw the world in nonreligious terms and fashioned a theological response.

That interpretation of the world has changed drastically in all but one of the "up-front" thinkers in this book. By the late 1960s a great change began to occur. Some of it was visible in the academy, where anthropologists like Clifford Geertz, Melford Spiro, Victor Turner and Mary Douglas came up with a much different picture of the human condition, whether in the "primitive" or "sophisticated" worlds. To be present to the world, Merleau-Ponty had said, was to be "condemned to meaning." People were not those sunny, agnostic, secular folk described by Bonhoeffer and Harvey Cox. They were metaphysical shoplifters, snatching anything that offered great gobs of meaning wherever they could get it. Sociologists like Thomas Luckmann and others in the chain of Talcott Parsons and, before him, Max Weber and Emile Durkheim, saw society itself as drenched in religious meanings. Parsons said that the human in culture could not sustain a world in which everything "just happens." He or she must endow joys and sorrows, fortunes and misfortunes with meaning.

The social thinkers also began to note how potent religion was in social binding. Harold Isaacs in *Idols of the Tribe* connected religion with ethnicity-culture-race in a blend that was producing the wars of our time. Everywhere, on a massive scale, people were gathering themselves together in groups informed by religious symbols. Together they protected their identities, their power and their place in the light of these symbols. And they used them "over against" others. If this was the case in Shi'ite Islam—the Iranian revolution had occurred before the authors wrote their contributions to this volume—it was also evident almost anywhere in Africa, in the attachment of Catholic symbols to social revolution in Latin America, in Hindu-Muslim battles on the Asian subcontinent, in Jewish-Muslim strife in the Middle East, in Protestant-Catholic battles in Northern Ireland. If religion was disappearing from the human story, its death rattles were certainly lethal; it was taking a lot of people down with it.

No, religion was not dying, say these theologians and the people with whom they associate or whom they read. Religion is part of the anthropological condition; so, at least, Thomas Luckmann taught them. It is essential to social formation. Even antireligious and atheist regimes like Marxist and Maoist ones develop at least pseudo-religions to legitimate their moves. Robert Heilbroner predicts that something of the same sort would occur should America undergo drastic social change. And also as other explanations failed, individuals also turned to religion.

To the theologians in the academic community a Distant Early Warning signal on which some of our authors report was the counterculture, under whatever names and flags it appeared. In this movement the sons and daughters of academicians, politicians and communicators turned their backs on the think tanks of planners and rationalists. For a few years they indulged in extravagant symbolic rejections of the movement from the Renaissance to the Great Society. They pursued magic through mind-expanding drugs, entertained the guru of the season in their communes and ravines, or, if they stayed near campuses, entertained literary forms of Eastern or occult religion.

As the counterculture faded, it was clear that it had helped create "plausibility structures" for many more at-home cultural forces. Among these were Hasidic Judaism, Christian Pentecostalism, Jesus movements, and a revival of evangelical-fundamentalist-charismatic religions of experience and authority. Left behind were the theologians and churches that had been asking: With how little baggage should modern spiritual pilgrims travel? Now people in culture wanted to be weighted down with every kind of spiritual option possible in their saddlebags.

In the opening section of the book we have posed three authors' visions; two of them agree in general with each other, though they may respond in different ways. Peter Berger, who a decade ago first read many of these signs of the times in *Rumors of Angels: Signals of Transcendence in the Modern World* appears here with a frank critique of the secular paradigm and those who live with it. Over against it he shows the values for Christian theology of an open engagement with other religions. He may have been growing ever more conservative politically, writes Berger, but his theological move has to look increasingly liberal in classic senses of the term. Langdon Gilkey, the most notable chronicler and critic of the "secular theology" in the mid-1960s now admits that he then tailored more of his own thinking to the secular outlook than he now likes to remember. He has since seen a great loss of faith in science and reason and a quickening of interest again in the sacred, in the religious evidences in the world around the theologian.

Since Gilkey does his writing across the hall from my own office, I had a chance to ask him about his essay as soon as it came from his typewriter. "A hundred years from now, which era or epoch will be easier for people to understand: how things were in 1965—the secular summit—or in 1980, a symbol of the loss of faith in science and reason, Renaissance and Enlightenment, and an embrace of religiousness?"

"Oh, 1980," was Gilkey's instant reply. He may be partly wrong, as most theologians were wrong in 1965. But the readiness of his reply indicates how deep he thinks the current revolt against the secular trajectory is.

Now, lest readers think that the whole theological world is unanimous, we have posed over against Berger and Gilkey someone who does an exact opposite reading of the times. Carl Henry, president in 1981 of the American Theological Society, no stranger to this series, and the best-known theologian of the renewed evangelical movement of our half-century in America, believes that secularity and humanism are still in the saddle, still winning, still posing the issues. Is he "living somewhere else" than the other authors in this book? On what planet does he live?

Are all evangelicals like him? This book cannot settle the issue. Certainly in militant fundamentalism, off to Henry's right, there is a great amount of polemics against "secular humanists," the scapegoats in the present politicization of evangelism. It may be that younger evangelicals would read the world more the way Berger and Gilkey and all our other authors do. But I have heard middle-aged Clark Pinnock say that he thinks Enlightenment secularity is alive, well and dominant. Could it be that evangelicals, having felt themselves excluded from the academy as liberals were not, bear resentments or have distortions of vision as to what it is about? Or, let us ask, may they be seeing the world around them more accurately than our other authors?

If Henry's reading is different, so is his solution. The note in these essays is one of "poignancy," for example, for Nathan Scott; "pathos" for Frederick Buechner; a kind of passivity for Gilkey, and limited expectations for the rest. Not much hubris made its way into these writings, and there seem to be few steppers-forward with a Bold New Vision for the age. Henry shares much of that sense of loss and even defeat about "his" evangelical movement. This is supposed to be its time of triumph, given its gains in popularity, support and cultural prominence. But it did not turn out right theologically, he notes. It is internally divided, distracted, directionless.

Henry gives much away when he complains that it is evangelicals who keep criticizing his kind of synthesis as "rationalistic." He who spends more passion on the Bible than any other author in this book, and who makes biblical authority the issue for the 1980s, does come on as the most at home with Renaissance-Enlightenment-scientific-rationalistic thought. The American evangelical movement as it took shape in Henry's generation was much given over to Aristotle, scholasticism and the Scottish Enlightenment's "common sense" realism. Could it be that Henry, who is completing a six-volume systematic theology, is building a magnificent edifice on a metaphysically condemned site? Or, for the authors who read the times differently than he, could he be tailoring an apology for an epoch that will be less moved by the rationalism to which his propositions point? I shall leave those questions as questions; the other authors are giving their own responses, though without reference to Henry. (Our authors do not get to compare notes with or respond to each other.)

All the other essays in the first part build on the "religious" paradigms of Berger and Gilkey and not on the "secular" model of Henry, though, of course, there are many variations as to how seriously religiousness and sacrality are to be taken. What the authors all have in common in this collection is their Christian standpoint, so they have to ask what Christians do as they formulate their witness to the word and action of God in a religious as opposed to a merely secular world. Their responses tend to pick up syncretic notes; they are not afraid to relate openly to, or to borrow from, other religions. Christianity derives from a history witnessed to in a Scripture that begins with Hebrew writings that occur in response to Yahweh. But Yahweh does not act independently of culture, and students of the Hebrew Scriptures keep finding in them evidences of syncretism. Yes, there was repudiation of the Baalim, and the prophets railed against what today we would call idolatry. But the rites and symbols, the stories and events of the people of Israel, picked up as much as they dropped from the Canaanite environment.

The New Testament is also not just the story of a simple Jesus dropped down from heaven and untinged by his environment. It is impossible to make sense of the Gospels apart from intertestamental developments in the language of apocalypticism. Christians picked up and dropped elements from "the religion of the Jews," their ancestors and cousins and selves at once. And the New Testament letters show an at-homeness with the very Greek and Roman cultures from which the authors also wanted to distance themselves. The language of their formulation, the thought patterns, the rites all reflect something of a world that included Stoics and mystery religions and apocalypticisms.

From biblical times to the present, Christians have absorbed much even as they have distanced themselves from religions around them. The Mbiti article here is a voice from within a culture that was not shaped by Christianity. He shows how from his viewpoint the missionaries did not bring a faith but found one, found many, in Africa, and grafted Christianity onto them. Where the newcomers were unwilling to graft, the Africans did so without benefit of clergy and through free enterprise. The Western writers pretty much agree with Mbiti's view.

This is not the first time that the notes of syncretism and universalism have been uttered on Christian soil. But the utterance runs counter to the language of the previous generations in theology. Hendrik Kraemer was only the most extreme writer in the era of Karl Barth as he rejected "native" religions in the face of Christianity's crucial and prophetic word. Until the final third of the 20th century the missionary impulse for Catholicism was more one of supplanting than supplementing.

Yet change occurred in Catholicism, too. *Nostra Aetate*, the Second

Vatican Council's word about world religions, is gentle, empathic, responsive, anything but repudiative. Like the theologians in this book, the church would itself regard spiritual stirrings and strivings beyond the Christian orbit with some appreciation. That Council document drew on Catholic latencies, like the Augustinian theme of "common grace," and legitimated them in a new generation.

Paul van Buren, in one of the more surprising changes of mind in this volume and decade, sheds the image of himself as someone who had linguistic problems in speaking of God at all. Now he has a new confidence that we can speak of God, but he sees the Christian voice being more responsive to Islam and Eastern religions. Yet most of his energies are clearly going into a restitution of conversation with Jews. His own program reaches back behind a breach effected by around 70 C.E. And it is informed by a reading, perhaps a creative misreading, of his mentor, Karl Barth.

Recently an organization of neo-conservatives was developed in America to put up billboards in praise of the West. The sponsors feel that there has been a treason of the intellectuals, who talk down the West and talk up other cultures. That organization would find fair game among our theologians. All of them are convinced Christians and, even if uneasily, want to remain in the sphere of witness to Jesus Christ. But they are anything but triumphalist about this, and want to recognize others and to learn. James M. Gustafson intends to remain "theocentric," but not in a crabbed, provincial way. John Hick is very explicit about what he is learning from other faiths, and more than any other of our authors tends to relativize Christian witness.

Such writers can hardly be accused of going with the *Zeitgeist*. The mood and spirit of the times call for a new fundamentalist, tribal, constrictive outlook. The day of the United Nations and United World Federalism and the World Council of Churches seems to have passed. The images of global village and spaceship earth are utterly unfashionable. The New Beginning in politics has us asserting that "We're Number One," that other nations are our "backyard," and that the West will rise again. These are days for "One Way" and "One Book," of xenophobia and ethnocentrism, also in religion. The theologians here want to enjoy their own faith and culture, but they want to be responsive theologically to other ways and witnesses. They may be reading the signs wrong, or responding incorrectly, but they cannot be accused of wanting to ride the waves.

In fact, the more I worked with these essays, the more it occurred to me that if these be liberals and if liberals are to sell out to their culture, then these are strange liberals with bizarre responses. What they have is not very marketable in a tribal time. They are really asking for an epochal shift in human consciousness at a time when the Iranian Revolution as a negative symbol—"They've got their ideology and we need ours"—and the returned Iranian hostages or the American Olympic Hockey team minister to the need to fortify an imperium apart. This theological shift instead asks people to combine their own commitment with civility, their own conviction with responsiveness. I know of no place in the world where such a vision is winning, where people are today more generous or empathic about others. I know of no "liberal" religious force that is triumphing against the grain of the times. These theologians, if they are right, must feel lonely, must work against all odds. And the very fundamentalists who might scorn them for playing into the "spirit of the times" are the ones who have the Zeitgeist in their pocket. Any market tester can prove that instantly.

In several other respects these theologians run against the stream. They write after the 1970s, a decade in which spiritual introversion and privatism in matters of faith were the top consumer items. Yet David Tracy and others call for a fresh understanding of "publicness," and for a public theology. Religious promoters, whether in cults or the electronic church, make their way successfully by evading hermeneutical issues. They need only invoke "the Leader says," or "the Bible says," to get converts. Yet the theologians here want to keep raising hermeneutical questions. Who interprets, from what standpoint, and what "pre-understanding" does the author impart and the reader bring?

In a time when it is politically fashionable to move quickly against defenders of the environment, and when it is certain that earth, sky and water will be despoiled for immediate economic purpose, these theologians invoke biblical doctrines of creation, philosophical views of process, and personal visions of stewardship. Lots of luck. No wonder in our "interlude" section Nathan Scott and Frederick Buechner, sensitive to literary nuance as they are, have personalized the role of the theologian in the face of loss, setback, defeat, death. . . .

A literary response of a simple and profound character comes through the voice of Elie Wiesel. He ponders the very value of words themselves when people make efforts to cross boundaries of unimaginable differences: "It's not because I don't speak that you won't understand me; it's because you won't understand me that I don't speak." But his world is not one of mere silence. He is now able to talk about some continuities with his own early life and with the power of the Sabbath and the sacred in Jewish contexts. And in doing so, he shows that his mind has indeed changed. In surprising ways, his breaking of silence, his speaking up, may cause some of us to change our own minds as well.

And there is another section of the book, about which much less need be said. This is the "Liberation" half, which some readers and reviewers are certain to dismiss as " '60ish," as "cultural lag." Certainly every author in it is as out of step with what is politically fashionable in North America as are the authors in the first half with that which is religiously marketable. The political leadership at the beginning of the 1980s by appointments and policies made clear that it was not going to be very responsive to calls for liberation in the Third World, or even to speak of the Third World at all. If Liberation means "human rights," the politicians decided to disdain claims made in the interests of that cause. There was to be a new fortress mentality, a new exclusivism of national claims, a new economic imperialism where America could get away with it.

Domestically, racial themes were to be submerged. Feminism was losing out to women themselves, when a new domesticity and a call for old submissive ways appeared as ideological themes against the Equal Rights Amendment. To speak up in the angry tones of black, Hispanic, native American or feminist movements of the 1960s would be implausible, should one wish to gain a hearing. I do detect a subdued, compromising note in the authors in this half. James M. Cone was certainly more exclusivistically "black" in the black power days than he is in this essay. Rosemary Ruether was promoting a socialist vision of the Christian faith already in the 1960s, as a complement to feminist liberation, but today there is less of the "anti-male" tone in her and other Christian feminist writings. They know that the communities out of which they write have lost considerable power to threaten or to make gains. They either are cultural laggards or they must believe in the intrinsic truth of what they are saying.

The essays by Harvey Cox and Robert McAfee Brown which open and close this section certainly play into the hands of those who say that the intellectuals, including the theologians, are contributing to the "decline of the West." Cox feels that the theological community is still too parochial, too provincial, and that the enterprise itself might be doomed. Brown is less ready to step out of the standpoint of his own culture, but is equally sure that American theologians have to be more expansive than before. Both are good-natured enough and have enough perspective to know that they cannot "jump out of their skins," as Cox puts it, but they do feel ill at ease in the present context of theology, no doubt even with that presented by the "pluralists" and "universalists" up front.

I find it somewhat easier to speak up for the "West" than they, though I hope not without criticism or awareness of the limits. As I read most of the liberationists quite properly defending themselves against the charge that their theology is Marxism, not biblically derived, I do keep noticing how much Marxist socialism willy-nilly *is* the alternate "system" to the capitalism they decry. That capitalism as a system in American hands produces outrage none of us can deny. The night before I wrote these later lines in this introduction, I watched a CBS portrayal of police brutality against Hispanics in McAllen, Texas. A hidden camera caught the images of police cruelly, viciously beating up on passive arrested Hispanics. Why? To show their macho to other police. It was a five-minute portrayal, just a glimpse to penetrate the media shield, just a moment that reminded me how seething I can become over an "unjust" traffic ticket, or even over being cut off in a supermarket or superhighway traffic lane. I experience slights. The minorities and poor of the world experience constant, sustained, depersonalizing, sub- and non- and anti-human and anti-Christian violence all the time. And my "system" is a complicitor in it.

But the liberationists do, it seems to me, here as elsewhere, make the socialisms and postrevolutionist alternatives too easy. We have yet to see in Africa, Asia or Latin America such revolutions that assure even as much freedom as people had before. And the revolutionaries are as adept at generating classes, privilege and violence as are the regimes they would replace. This is not to say that there is nothing creative in replacement of regimes, but only to remember that in the Christian scheme, the admonition "put not your trust in princes" or systems has to reach into all systems. We are learning not to trust "minority" regimes when they become "majority" powers and act against whites, northerners, westerners or whatever the former oppressors may be.

That note aside, I must say that these liberationists do run against all the tendencies of our time. They will not get a political hearing in America in much of the 1980s, and there are not many signs that the churches will hear them. There are exceptions. Some American Catholics in the northern continent are listening to the travail of their southern continental counterparts. Persecution of missionaries in right-wing as well as left-wing regimes awakens some Protestant evangelicals. But political fashion will work against foreign aid, sympathy for rising peoples, or human rights beyond our shores in the 1980s.

One might say that the proportions of this book are even distorting. Cox and Brown are probably correct in their implication that most theology is less mindful of the calls for liberation. I know that the neoconservative politicians who know anything about religion like to act as if mainline Catholic and Protestant seminaries are nests of liberation theology. Some of these politicians were themselves divines, and they carry memories of their own radicalism of the '60s into administration in the '80s—freezing their former colleagues into positions they may, together, once have held. These colleagues have moved on, and as politicians, now rightist, find it necessary to keep taking revenge against their own spiritual past by striking out at people who, they feel, did not "convert" radically enough to the new right.

Most theological schools of my acquaintance have only "a" liberation-minded feminist, or black, or Third-Worlder, or would-be any of the three. And that is it. The professional societies of theologians will schedule an occasional paper on the topic. But most of the concern now is technical: for texts, interpretation, hermeneutics, publicness, universalism-relativism-pluralism, and issues of the sort that are in the first half of the book. The two interests are by no means contradictory, and the authors in the two halves of this book have overlapping interests and often side with each other—witness Schubert Ogden's appreciative critique of liberation. But I am arguing that the liberationists, if they had some cultural tendencies on their side in the '60s, have few if any in the '80s. The Christian Century as an ecumenical and international journal, alert to ethnicity and peoplehood and issues of generation and gender, is probably more flexible and more open to theological currents of many sorts than are the typical academies, universities, seminaries, or church agencies. So giving over almost half of this book to the world that does not follow middle-class, male, Western models in theology might be slightly skewing. Think of it as equal time, as compensatory vigor against the odds. Do not think of the last half of the book as a kind of Gallup Poll of theologians, to certify the vision of neoconservatives that a bunch of Marxists have taken over Christian thought.

How representative, then, are our thinkers? There are some missing folk. Hans Küng and Edward Schillebeeckx, the two best-known Catholic theologians today, are friendly to our enterprises and "wish they could have contributed." However, both pleaded pressures of circumstance and both pointed to the fact that the Vatican has given them a bully pulpit elsewhere for all the world to hear or read them, as they defended themselves. Both of them share many of the presuppositions of the authors in the first part of this book. Had they been here, their work suggests, there might have been more attention to the figure of Jesus Christ. We could have done well with one of the "younger evangelical" theologians, who would have been a counterpoise to Henry's view, from within the camp. I miss a Paul Ricoeur here, for he more than any other Christian thinker I know is having a strong impact on philosophy in the academy and hermeneutics in the seminary. But he is a kind of hidden figure behind many of the essays. Every reader is likely to have a nominee or two who has been slighted here. This is not a popularity poll, but an assessment by editors and the people they consult. Who today demands a hearing by the quality of his or her achievement? Who represents a viewpoint that merits a hearing, even if our chosen writer is not a household name in Christian circles?

Not until the articles all came in and not until I read them all together did I realize how out of step they are. Not out of step in their vision of a religious world replacing the one thought to be secular, but in their calculation as to what to do in response. Far more marketable are the statements of those who meet the challenge of other religions by canceling them all out and building high walls around one's own. Dean Kelley opened the decade of the '70s with a book that showed how and why authoritarianisms, fanaticisms, exclusivisms, illiberalisms, and spitefulnesses were more attractive than responsive and dialogical forces. Which kinds of voices, those exemplified here or the strident, belligerent and successful ones, are more in continuity with Christian charters and intentions, and which will do more to build a humane world we shall have to let readers, and unfolding times, decide.

I

The Context
and the Issues:
Three Statements

PETER L. BERGER

From Secularity
to World Religions

To be asked to tell how one's mind has changed over a decade is an invitation to narcissism. To accept the invitation would seem to imply a quite solemn view of one's own importance. My incurably Lutheran sensibility tells me that such a view is sinful, and my even more incurable sense of the comic says that it is ridiculous. Still, after an initial hesitation, I accepted. I did so precisely because I believe that my mind is not so unusual for its peregrinations not to have some common utility. My experiences over the past ten years are, by and large, commonly accessible, and it seems to me that most of my conclusions could be arrived at by anybody.

Third World Influences

The time period suggested by *The Christian Century*'s series suits me very conveniently, at least as far as my thinking about religious matters is concerned. In 1969 my book *A Rumor of Angels* was published, and in 1979 my book *The Heretical Imperative.* In between, most of my work as a sociologist was directly concerned not with religion but with modernization and Third World development, as well as with the problem (which first preoccupied me in the Third World) of how sociological insights can be translated into compassionate political strategies.

Yet these sociological excursions, as it turned out, had an indirect effect on my thinking about religion. If I were asked for the most important experience leading from the one book to the other, I would have to say the Third World. In the 1960s I was preoccupied with the problems of secularity, and *A Rumor of Angels* was an attempt to overcome secularity from within. The Third World taught me how ethnocentric that preoccupation was: secularization is today a worldwide phenomenon, it is true, but one far more entrenched in North America and Europe than anywhere else, so that a more global perspective inevitably provides a more balanced view of the phenomenon. Conversely, the Third World impresses one with the enormous social force of religion. It is this very powerful impression that eventually led me to the conclusion, stated in *The Heretical Imperative,* that a new contestation with the other world religions should be a very high priority on the agenda of Christian theology.

As I understand my own thinking, it has not moved in a radical way during this period. The problems that have preoccupied me have shifted considerably, but my underlying religious and political positions have remained more or less the same. To the extent that I have moved, though, I have moved further to the "left" theologically and further to the "right" politically. This development has confused and also distressed some of my friends (though, needless to say, some have been cheered by what others found distressing).

Again, the Third World has been crucial for both movements of thought. It has given me empirical access to the immense variety and richness of human religion, and thus has made it impossible for me (once and for all, I believe) to remain ethnocentrically fixated on the Judeo-Christian tradition alone. I moved more radically in the 1950s and early 1960s in my thinking about religion (mainly, it seems in retrospect, under the impact of experiencing America after what John Murray Cuddihy has aptly called "the fanaticisms of Europe"), outgrowing the neo-orthodox positions of my youth and finally concluding that my thinking fitted best within the tradition of Protestant liberalism. But the personal as well as intellectual encounter with the Third World gave that liberalism a scope that I could not foresee earlier.

I can say with confidence that the human misery of Third World poverty and oppression has shocked me as deeply as it can anyone coming from the comfortable West, and I have been and continue to be fully convinced of the urgency of seeking alleviation for it. But my efforts to understand the causes of this misery and to conceive plausible strategies for overcoming it have impressed me with the utter fatuity of the alleged solutions advocated by the political "left." To be sure, this insight has not in itself been theologically productive, but it has prevented me from taking the currently fashionable route of doing theology by baptizing the empty slogans of this or that version of Marxism with Christian terminology.

Modified Views of Secularization

It so happens that, for me, the decade staked out by *The Christian Century* coincided with visits to Rome both at the beginning and the end. In 1969 I organized and chaired a conference there on behalf of the Vatican's Secretariat for Nonbelievers. It was a fascinating event, especially in the contacts it provided between members of the Roman ecclesiastical establishment and a somewhat wild assortment of scholars who had worked on the problem of secularization. The proceedings of the conference were subsequently published in a book aptly titled *The Culture of Unbelief.*

One incident from the conference that has stuck in my memory took place at a party. A leading Demochristian politician, very puzzled, asked a monsignor from the secretariat what this conference was all about. *"La secolarizzazione,"* replied the monsignor. *"Secolarizzazione,"* repeated the politician, then asked: "What is this?" The monsignor valiantly rose to the challenge and gave a rather adequate ten-minute summary. The crusty old gentleman of the Democrazia Christiana listened very carefully, then raised his hand and said in a firm voice: "We will not permit it!"

At the time, the remark impressed me as very funny. A few weeks later I went to Mexico, at the invitation of Ivan Illich—a trip that turned out to be decisive in concentrating my attention on the Third World. I remember telling Illich the story. He laughed, but he did not think it as funny as I did. Illich is often right (often, not always). In this instance, his finding the idea of prohibiting secularization less outrageous than I found it was wise.

In 1979 I was in Rome just as the Iranian revolution was breaking out. I watched the events in Iran on Italian television with a good deal of nervousness, as I was supposed to fly to India via Tehran. There were the vast masses of Khomeini followers, with their posters and banners, seemingly stretching to the horizon. And they kept chanting: *"Allahu akbar!"*—"God is great!" I had to think of that remark about secularization of a decade ago, and it did not seem funny at all. Indeed, a dramatic prohibition of secularization is exactly what Khomeini had in mind, and, whatever the eventual outcome of the Iranian revolution, it must be conceded that he has been rather successful in this undertaking thus far.

Certainly in the Islamic world, from the Atlantic Ocean to the China Sea, it is religion that offers a militant challenge to every form of secularity (including the Marxist one), and not the other way around. In the event, the turmoil in Iran forced me to change my travel plans and fly directly to India—my first visit there, one that immersed me more completely than ever before in a non-Western religious culture. And while Hinduism, for many reasons, does not exhibit the dynamism of contemporary Islam, it too most assuredly is not behaving as the idea of secularization I held in the 1960s would have predicted.

The Third World is not the only reason why I have modified my earlier view of secularization. There has been impressive evidence of religious resurgence in North America. There has also been a significant religious revival in at least certain sectors of Soviet society, all the more significant because of a half-century of determined and sophisticated repression. This does not mean, as some have suggested, that secularization theory has been simply a mistake. But one can now say, I think, that both the extent and the inexorability of secularization have been exaggerated, even in Europe and North America, and much more so in other parts of the world. In itself, this is no more than a revision of a sociological thesis under the pressure of empirical evidence. As such, it is theologically neutral. Yet, inevitably (it seems to me, at any rate), it suggests that the problem of secularity is not quite as interesting for the Christian mind as many of us used to think. After all, it is one thing to engage in intellectual contestation with a phenomenon deemed to be the wave of the future, quite another to do so with one of many cultural currents in play in the contemporary world.

The Crisis of Modernity

Sociologically speaking, the phenomenon of secularization is part and parcel of a much broader process—that of modernization. In the context of Christian theology, of course, the dialogue with secularity (which, I suppose, one can simply describe as the mind-set resulting from secularization) has been pretty much the same as the dialogue with modernity—or with that well-known figure "modern man," whom Rudolf Bultmann and others conceived to be incapable of believing the world view of the New Testament.

Speaking sociologically again, there are good reasons for thinking that modernity, and modern secularity with it, is in a certain crisis today. It became clear to me in the Third World that modernization is not a unilinear or an inexorable process. Rather, from the beginning, it is a process in ongoing interaction with countervailing forces which may be subsumed under the heading of countermodernization. It is useful, I think, to look at secularization in the same way—as standing in ongoing interaction with countersecularizing forces. The details of this relationship cannot be spelled out here. Suffice it to say that countermodernization and countersecularization can be observed not only in the Third World but also in the so-called advanced industrial societies, those of both the capitalist and the socialist varieties.

All of this strongly suggests a shift in theological attention, away from the much-vaunted engagement with modern consciousness and its theoretical products. It should be stressed that this is not to say that some of the latter products do not continue to offer theological challenges. I suspect that this is particularly true of developments in the physical sciences, those prime products of modernity, but this is an area in which I'm woefully ignorant and into which I'm therefore most reluctant to venture. Also, it is clear that, theories and world views apart, the modern situation continues to pose ethical problems of great gravity—but that is not quite the same as what the dialogue with "modern man" was to be about.

I would also like it to be clear that, in saying that modern consciousness is not as interesting theologically as many have thought (or not as interesting as it once was—for example, in the 19th century, when Christian theology had to deal with the challenge of modern historical thought), I'm not in the least implying some sort of antimodern stance. There is much of this around today (for instance, in the radical wing of the ecology movement), and some of it is quite appealing, but it will not stand up under rigorous scrutiny. It is not so much that we cannot go back (there is no law that says that the clock cannot be turned back—it can be, it has been), but that the human costs of demodernizing would be horrendously large. Take just one item: one of the most dramatic consequences of modernity has been the marked decline in infant mortality. I don't see how any conceivably viable assessment of modernity could conclude that this has been a bad thing.

The Compulsion to Choose

Already in the early 1960s, when I was working with Thomas Luckmann on new ways of formulating the sociology of knowledge, it had become clear to us that secularization and pluralism were closely related phenomena. The root insight here is that subjective certainty (in religion as in other matters) depends upon cohesive social support for whatever it is that the individual wants to be certain about. Conversely, the absence or weakness of social support undermines subjective certainty—and that is precisely what happens when the individual is confronted with a plurality of competing world views, norms or definitions of reality. I continue to think that this insight is valid. Increasingly, however, it has seemed to me that, of the two phenomena, pluralism is more important than secularization. Put differently: the modern situation would present a formidable challenge to religion even if it were, or would come to be, much less secularized than it now is.

Competition means having to choose. That is true in a market of material commodities—this brand as against that, this consumer option as against that. Whether one likes it or not, the same compulsion to choose is the result of a market of world views—this faith or this "life style" against that. I have called this crucial consequence of pluralism "the heretical imperative," and I have tried in my recent book of that title to analyze different theological responses to this rather uncomfortable situation. Again, I do not perceive my thinking as having changed dramatically on these matters. But at least two accents have changed. First, it is much clearer to me now why the theological method (not necessarily any of the contents) of classical Protestant liberalism, with its stress on experience and reasonable choice, is the most viable one today. And second, because of my previously mentioned encounter with the Third World, I now have a much broader notion of the range of relevant choices in religion.

As a result of this perspective on the religious situation and its theological possibilities, I have for quite a while found myself in a sort of two-front position. Fronting the theological "right," I'm convinced that any attempts to reconstruct old certainties, as if "the heretical imperative" could be ignored, are futile. This conviction makes it impossible for me to seek alignment with any form of orthodoxy or neo-orthodoxy. On the other hand, I see no more promise in the "left" strategies of trying to make Christianity plausible by secularizing its contents, no matter whether this "secularization from within" (one of Luckmann's helpful terms) is done by means of philosophy, psychology or political ideology. All these strategies are finally (and, indeed, rather soon) self-liquidating, as they rob the religious enterprise of whatever plausibility it still has within the consciousness of individuals.

Incidentally, this does not mean that I have no empathy with either the "right" or the secularizing-"left" positions. The former was the position of my youth, in the form of a sort of muscular Lutheranism, and (if nothing else) the nostalgias of middle age assure a lingering empathy. As to the latter position, it is not just a matter of "some of my best friends" and all that. More important, anyone who lives and works in a modern secular milieu undergoes every day the same cognitive tensions that move people toward this position, and a high degree of empathy is thereby given almost automatically.

In this connection, a word should be said about an event with which I was associated, the so-called Hartford Appeal of 1975—a statement that forcefully repudiated various secularizing trends in contemporary theological thought. It was widely regarded as a neo-orthodox manifesto. Whatever may have been the understanding of others connected with the event, this was not the way I understood it. For me, Hartford delineated what separated me from those to the "left" of the liberal position I espoused. Such delineation continues to be necessary, I believe (though, in retrospect, it is debatable whether the style of the Hartford Appeal was the most suitable). For me, however, delineation with regard to the theological "right" is equally important, and I hope that *The Heretical Imperative* has now fulfilled this purpose.

The worst thing about being in the middle is not that one is shot at from both sides. In this instance that is not so bad, as there are a lot of people in the same location. More disturbing is the thought that a *via media*, especially in religion, is always beset with tepidness. And that has indeed been one of the recurring qualities of Protestant liberalism. True enough, but I don't think that this is a necessary quality. Every nuanced, reflected-upon position is in danger of appearing tepid in comparison with the self-confident postures of those who claim certainty. It is important to understand the illusionary character of the self-confident postures, at which point mellowness acquires its own certainty, more quiet perhaps than that of the Barthians, say, or of the Christian revolutionaries, but also more enduring.

The Act of Preaching

Speaking of Barthians, there is one question that concerned them from the beginning, indeed that first motivated Karl Barth himself in his early theological thinking: "How does one preach that?" The question is a crucial one, not only for those who are vocationally charged with preaching, but also for those (including myself) who are committed to the public reaffirmation of the Christian tradition. It is many years now since, after one (very happy) year at the Lutheran Theological Seminary in Philadelphia, I drew back from the ministry as my own vocational goal. All biographical decisions are murky, but this one was essentially simple: I felt that I could not be a Lutheran minister unless I could fully assent to the definition of the faith as stated in the Lutheran confessions, and I drew back from this role because I doubted whether I could give such unqualified assent. In other words, I felt that I, for one, could not preach "that." I do not regret this long-ago decision, but it is relevant to these observations that today I would arrive at a different conclusion. If "that" is now understood as being the liberal position alluded to above, then I'm deeply convinced that it can indeed be preached—and, given the call to do that, I'm convinced that I could.

The reason for this conclusion is also essentially simple: I believe that at the core of the Christian tradition is truth, and this truth will reassert itself in every conceivable contestation—be it with the multiform manifestations of modern secularity, or with the powerful traditions of Asian religion awaiting theological engagement. To be sure, no one who honestly enters into such a contestation emerges the way one entered; if one did, the contestation was probably less than honest. In the act of reflection, every honest individual must be totally open, and this also means open-ended.

The act of preaching is different. Here the individual does not stand before the tradition in the attitude of reflection but deliberately enters into it and reaffirms the truth that he has discovered through it, without thereby forgetting or falsifying the fruits of reflection.

There is no way of predicting the movements of the spirit. I have often thought that even a person equipped with all the tools of modern social science would have been hard put to predict the Reformation, say, at the onset of the 16th century. I will not make a prediction here, but I will make a guarded statement: it is possible that out of the contestations of our time will emerge preaching voices of great and renewed power. There is a kind of stillness now, and has been for quite some time. It is possible that the stillness will be followed by thunder. We do not know this. We are not supposed to know. But the possibility is worth a cautious hope, and perhaps even a gamble of faith.

LANGDON GILKEY

Theology for a Time of Troubles

It was some 16 years ago that I was graciously invited (challenged?) by
The Christian Century to write one of the articles in the series "How I Am
Making Up My Mind" ("Dissolution and Reconstruction in Theology,"
February 3, 1965). Now, 16 years later, writing for the awesome series
"How My Mind Has Changed," I prefer, if I may, to say "How My Mind
Is Changing." Instead of having the sensation of motion followed by
present rest and clarity ("has changed"), I am now overwhelmed by the
sense of being theologically still in passage, as yet unsolidified and un-
clear. Whatever is here in motion is only beginning or embarking on its
journey; it is not at all completing or fulfilling it. What is more, I have the
feeling of being in quite another sort of passage than that which dominated my experience 16 years ago.

Gasping for Breath

Since this all sounds like a fairly heady trip, let me begin with the
contrast I note between the sense of change characterizing the present,
and the upheavals and radical changes experienced in the middle '60s
and recorded in that earlier article. In each case (1965 and 1981) it is evident (and somewhat embarrassing) that my sense of theological dislocation is hardly a matter of my own new insight or innovation, but one of a
somewhat panicky, sloppy and inept *reaction* to external events, to massive and threatening cultural and historical changes that, quite against
my will, force on me a different procedure, a different viewpoint, a different set of questions—a different theology.

Theology (at least as I do it) is hardly serene, self-generated, or in
control; it is barely able to get the ship in before the unexpected storm, or
the clothes in out of the rain—and it is always gasping for breath! I was,
therefore, relieved to note that Reinhold Niebuhr, in speaking of one of

his own articles in this series (1959–60), also suggested a title expressive of the experience of reactive passivity: "How My Mind Has Reacted to World Events."

The sense of upheaval, of radical change and of the need for a new mode in theology was deep in 1965. I referred in that article to "shifting ice," "the sudden thaw of theological certainties," and "rushing depths of dark water." The problem raised for us as theologians or preachers came from renewed awareness of the reality, power and value of the "secular," as we liked to call it—that is, of the scientific, technological, pragmatic, liberal and democratic culture that made up the "modern world" in which we theologians lived. This was a serious *problem* for us, if not a lethal menace, because this culture asked empirical questions about the meaning and the validity of our religious language—questions that were embarrassing to our early theological certainties (mostly "biblical theological" certainties). And this secular culture challenged a church (and most theologians) concerned with private and personal, "existential" problems to become active and involved in the more serious public issues of a segregated and an imperialistic America.

In comparison with this "modern" world with its demanding cognitive criteria and its high social ideals, the traditional religions seemed anachronistic and outdated, empty and uncertain, narcissistic and undemanding—and incurably white and bourgeois. Most of us felt this contrast as a deep challenge, and it was a challenge precisely because the secular that threatened our theology and even our religion represented such a compelling *lure* to us—in fact, as we recognized, it represented in many respects a major, or *the* major, aspect of our own self addressing us.

A Secular World

Consequently, many of us spent the next decade working through an answer to the question of the meaning of religious language in terms of ordinary experience, in terms of a "revision" or "re-presentation" of the Christian tradition "intelligible to modern minds," and worked on formulating an appropriate and strong political theology. Even if the "God is dead" theology has itself long since been interred, these problems which a secular culture poses to religious meanings have by no means vanished. That same secular world with its nagging empirical criteria of meaning and validity remains in power in academia and among the middle and especially the professional classes—and we who try to do theology are still ourselves very much a part of that same world.

Correspondingly, the questions of justice, liberation and peace represent the predominant moral issues of our present cultural life. Thus in our present situation the hermeneutical problem (how traditional words, concepts and symbols are to be interpreted intelligibly in our cultural present) on the one hand remains *the* problem for those concerned with the theoretical issues of theology, and on the other the issue of liberation represents the center for those concerned more with the meaning of theology in life and in action. And there is hardly any constructive theologian worth her or his salt who does not try to do both.

Although these issues arising in the '60s still remain central for theology, the world has meanwhile changed and (as usual) changed radically. The fundamental balance of things that created that former set of problems has itself shifted, uncovering some new and quite different issues. I find myself seeing quite a new scene when I look out the same windows, sniffing different winds from another direction, and thus sensing quite different theological problems moving rapidly toward me over the same old terrain.

Questioning the Scientific Method

The first element of the new scene may be called the "re-evaluation of the secular"; in this context, by "secular" I again refer to a culture that depends primarily on the empirical, scientific consciousness and that therefore tends to negate any sort of mystical consciousness. Those who like brisker language might wish to define this new scene not as one merely of re-evaluation but as the beginning of the "disintegration of the secular culture"—but that judgment is probably quite premature. What is clear, however, is the fact of its reassessment or re-evaluation.

And the first thing to be re-evaluated has been the claim of the scientific method to represent *the* method of knowledge solely able to relate cognitively to reality—a claim that seemed quite dominant and secure in the '50s and the early '60s. In its place has come a new consciousness of the ambiguity and the inadequacy, even the distorting effect, of that method if it alone contributes to or fashions our fundamental view of reality. It was perhaps the central thrust of the counterculture of the late '60s to repudiate this claim of the scientific consciousness (cf. Theodore Roszak's analysis), and to question the ability of technology to provide, via an expanding industrial and consumer culture, a creative basis for human fulfillment. Since then, for a number of reasons (air and water pollution, health concerns ignored and in fact unknown by scientific medicine, ecological issues), this questioning of the omnicompetence of the scientific method to uncover *the* truth, and of the creative value of technological "progress," has deepened and spread and now penetrates much further into the culture as a whole.

The Reappearance of the Religious

Corresponding to this new sense of the ambiguity (not the invalidity or inutility) of the scientific and technological base of the culture has come what could be termed the reappearance of the religious. That religious concerns, beliefs and institutions might linger on for some time in a secular age had been ruefully admitted by the children of Enlightenment humanism. But that these concerns would reappear in fresh and vigorous power, not only in the midst of a modern scientific and industrial culture but as a conscious and relevant reaction to the tensions and dilemmas created by that culture—that was not at all expected.

This is precisely what has happened, and happened in ways that caught theological as well as secular savants by surprise. For what has reappeared in strength has not been at all the kind of mainline, liberal and "modern" religion (*Christian Century* and University of Chicago religion!) designed to be intelligible to and appropriate for a secular world. On the contrary, it has been precisely those forms of religion believed in one way or another to be antithetical to a secular world, and so vulnerable to "the acids of modernity," that have sprouted up everywhere and have grown at an astounding rate; namely, fundamentalist religion of every variety; ecstatic, charismatic religion; esoteric, cultic religion; mystical, otherworldly religion; religious sectarianism that "opts out" of society, its customs and its responsibilities—not to mention every possible variety of the occult.

And the further interesting thing is that the forms of religion that are more bizarre or alien to modern Western "scientific" culture—astrology, occultism, Zen, yoga, Sufism—appeal to the "intelligentsia" and so ironically tend to cluster about our contemporary university centers (the remaining seats of that culture). Meanwhile the less alien varieties—that is, fundamentalist or ecstatic forms of our own traditional faiths—abound amid the nonintellectual portions of our cultural life, in "Middle America."

New Questions

The religious as an authentic, self-evidencing, powerful and healing aspect of experience, yet often also a demonic and destructive one, has made its appearance in every conceivable form in the midst of an "advanced" culture, baffling and alarming both the established secularism of academia and the established religious forces of the ecclesia. Former nagging questions of the meaning and verifiability of religious language—a language thought to be totally inapplicable to ordinary experience—now seemed themselves to be anachronistic questions, reflective of ivory-tower intellectuals or academics quite out of touch with vast ranges of ordinary experience.

The questions about religion and public life, those calling for "public" discussion, are no longer questions of the verifiability of religious speech but concern quite other issues: methods of understanding and describing the religious realities, old and new, that we see appearing around us; useful criteria for assessing these religions and for defining and comprehending this new set of powers in our public life; and ways of protecting vital religious groups from the excesses of the public reaction to them, and protecting the public from the excesses of powerful religious groups—hardly questions a secular culture had thought it would have to take seriously!

The religious dimension of experience appears to have re-presented itself in full force, in all its historic creativity, in answer to real social and psychological needs, and in all its historic explosive and demonic power. One could point as further evidence to the manifest "religious" characteristics of the two dominant contemporary secular ideologies: communism and liberal, democratic capitalism. These characteristics include their concern for commitment by their adherents; their concentration on questions of heresy or revisionism; their endless missionary propaganda; their global claims for their own values, for their unique place in history, for their "God-given" destiny for all of humanity. Whatever the case may be with "God," religion and the religious are not dead in our present cultural or political situation.

On the contrary, most counterfactual of all now appears the "secular" confidence, so common a year ago, that as a scientific and democratic culture unfolded, religion would gradually dissipate as an effective force in personal and social life alike. As a consequence, the "secular" understanding both of society and of the religious must be reassessed. This appearance of the religious in the midst of secular society—and in forms far different from our traditional religious communions—raises, of course, as well a host of vital theological issues that cannot be ignored: What is the relation of Christianity (or of Judaism) to these new and old religious communities? What is the relation of Christianity to the "religious dimension" of a social order? Granted that a purely "secular" social order now appears as more a wish-fulfillment than a possible reality, what kind of social order can really *encompass* the religious in all its creativity, its uneasy pluralism, and its demonic force?

The second and certainly more important element in what I have termed the "re-evaluation of the secular" is the manifestation of the *precariousness* in future history, if not the imminent mortality, of that secular culture. To itself, as it developed in the 18th and 19th centuries, and to its loyal descendants (at least, in the Anglo-Saxon West) through the first half of the 20th century, that culture defined and was thought to be identical to "modernity"; as a result, it was believed that this same culture would shape all the continually developing forms of modernity; that is, would represent the dominant culture not only of the immediate future but of the distant future as well. Would not of a certainty science, technology and industrialism develop, mature and so only increase in extent? And would not the accompanying cultural values of that scientific society—pragmatic openness; tolerance; freedom of inquiry, of belief and of decision; the democratic process, and self-control—also increase? And with an increase of democracy and goods, would not equality and justice also steadily grow in strength?

To be sure, Continental Europe—or some Europeans—felt by the end of World War I that it was experiencing the gradual disintegration, if not the final end, of its culture. But Americans had not experienced that war in that way; and thus our confidence—on whatever terms—in the future stability and even expansion of our own scientific, technological, industrial liberal and democratic society remained unabated even through the brief challenge to that culture's domination represented by the rise of fascism.

Again, to be sure, the appearance of fascism in a highly advanced society effectively dissolved the easy (but to us now strange) identification of advancement in civilization with an advancement in morals—an identification intrinsic to the conception of historical progress. But the subsequent defeat of fascism seemed to have rescued our culture, to have given it a new start—and thus covered over once more the possibility of that culture's ending, the incipient mortality of the democratic and liberal culture which fascism had challenged. In any case, it has remained for subsequent decades to herald that approaching end, to exhibit that possible mortality in ever clearer fashion. For what these decades have done is to uncover internal and yet unknown contradictions in that culture, and unheeded external threats to it, which now seem to portend clearly its objective loss of dominance, its internal disintegration and transformation. Those contradictions and threats might well in the end result in the culture's ultimate demise.

The Threat to Ecology

These remarks do not represent a prediction. Nothing in history is certain or determined. But it is simply the case that in a "time of troubles" (to borrow Toynbee's phrase), wisdom, courage and virtue must abound lest the mere possibility of demise be transformed, through our frantic reaction to its menacing appearance, into a virtual certainty.

The first manifestation of this dilemma or contradiction leading to possible mortality is the ecological crisis—the threat which an expanding technological and industrial culture poses to the nature system and the natural resources on which all life depends, including the life of a technological and industrial society itself. Unless that technological, industrial establishment is radically controlled—thereby effecting a transformation of vast areas of our political, economic and social life—the culture has a very good chance of destroying itself through increasingly inadequate supplies, through endless conflicts for those ever scantier materials, and through the systems of control and authority necessary to cope with each of these dangers.

The problem is essential and not accidental for the culture, and thus it is deep, lethal. That is, it arises precisely from what has been most characteristic and creative about modern civilization: its dynamically accumulating knowledge and technology, its expanding industrial system and its emphasis on egalitarian consumerism. It is these that have together caused, and continue to cause, "advanced" culture's menace to our common resources and to our natural environment as a whole. This menace threatens what is noble as well as what is "earthy" in the culture's life: its emphasis on personal individuality and freedom, its democratic processes and rights, its tolerance of variety and pluralism, as well as its high levels of bodily security and comfort, its affluence and its constant hopes for material improvement.

The Loss of Western Dominance

The second harbinger of possible mortality for Western civilization and culture has been the dramatic shift in the past few decades in the relative global power and influence of that culture. From the time the Turks challenged Vienna in 1456 to the Japanese attack in 1941 (nearly 500 years), no non-Western power had been able effectively to challenge a major Western power, let alone the whole of the West. Western powers challenged and vanquished one another, to be sure; but the entire globe was theirs to take unless they were checked by one of themselves. Thus their arms, as well as their ideas, their modes of existing and operating, their symbols and values, conquered almost everything in their way. (No *wonder* this expanding Europe thought that history represented progress!)

Since 1945, this situation has altered dramatically and with incredible speed: now only one Western power remains among the four major powers, and no European power any longer by itself enjoys the level of a world power. Europe has begun to acclimatize itself to this precipitous descent. America, being the remaining inheritor of Western world power, has yet even to try to realize that domination is no longer a possibility or a possible goal, that world power must be shared, not only with other groups with their own interests but with groups holding quite other cultural and value systems. And thus that the continuation of our power—and that of our forms of cultural order—is precarious at best.

The fact of this vast reduction in our relative power is presently writ large on countless world events; it is felt every day by Americans; and it is expressed in a wide variety of frustrated, angry, anxious and "macho" ways. The concrete policies of particular administrations can no doubt slow or accelerate this massive historical trend marking the end of an era of Western dominance; no one American administration, however, has created that trend, nor probably can any fundamentally alter its course.

Courage or Panic

As with the trend represented by the unraveling ecological crisis, policy cannot stop the process, but policy still can be rational or irrational, moral or immoral, and so creative or destructive. We as a nation might (at least in principle) face dwindling common resources by creating rational and fair modes of common control, of mutual sharing and of gradually effective methods of redistribution—*or* we can react to the same trend by trying to commandeer those scant resources, by fighting with our rivals and by imposing an authoritarian discipline.

Correspondingly, we can face the loss of dominant authority and power with wisdom and serenity, with an eye to the just aims of newly emerging forces, and, above all, with resolution in maintaining our most creative traditional ideals. *Or* we can seek to retain our power and affluence intact; support "friendly" dictators here, there and everywhere; and thus corrupt our ideals into an ideology defending remaining islands of privilege, and in so doing render those ideals irrelevant to and meaningless for the newly emerging world.

Human freedom in history never means the freedom to change the fundamental trends of an epoch—England could not have *willed* to remain a "great power" in the second half of the 20th century. But still, within the unfolding of a trend, freedom is faced with momentous political choices, choices representing reason or unreason, courage or panic, generosity and compassion or aggressive and destructive sin. An old culture, like an old bear, can suddenly whiff the dank odor of its own mortality; and then it is tempted, and tempted deeply, to sacrifice its ideals for the preservation of its life—and thus to hasten the very demise in history that it fears so much.

A Worldly Word
Clearly, the secular culture of which we are a part—and to which we rightly seek to adapt the gospel—is *itself* undergoing the deepest of crises. In such "times of troubles," problems mount to seemingly insoluble proportions; fears, basic anxieties and panic increase; conflicts become more lethal; "civil religions" begin to come apart—and a process of self-destruction on every level—economic, political, social and ideological—may well ensue. In such times, questions of policy are, of course, uppermost and in the forefront of attention: economic, political, social and international policy. But within these questions, behind them and through them are woven *moral* and *religious* issues of vast import to every political, economic and social decision.

It is, then, to the moral and religious issues of this coming time of troubles—appearing already but promising more to come!—that Christian theology and preaching (as well as academic reflection) must *also* address themselves. For not only are we theologians and our universities part of this common cultural world and so responsible to address it, but our churches and classrooms are in that world, too. It is the people in the churches and in the classes who will share in these common decisions, and it is their communities that will make them.

Theology and preaching must, therefore, *address* their responsible Word to the world, as well as *adapt* their Word to it. This Word is, of course, Christian in its sources. But it is worldly, timely and deeply public in its relevance, and it must be said and be heard: a word of *obligation* in relation to each moral issue as it arises; a word of the *retrieval* of the culture's most creative ideals and institutions; a word of *judgment* on the culture's present and potential sins; a word of *forgiveness* whenever it is repentent; a word of *promise* and so of confidence (in God, if not in itself) for the future.

Clearly, more than an expertise in theological or hermeneutical method is here required. Ethical issues of justice, liberation and sharing come starkly to the fore in all relevant reflection and speaking. The question of God's providence as the principle of historical judgment on the one hand and of new future possibilities on the other is a requirement for any theology fit for the time. And the confidence in the divine mercy and care for a world in agony—known through the incarnation and the cross—must be continually reiterated.

As a final note, let us recall how important it was that Augustine, contemplating the dismemberment of the glorious Roman Imperium, conceived of the gospel in such terms that it *transcended* that Hellenistic culture to which he had also so deftly and profoundly *adapted* it. It was precisely out of that transcendence affected by Augustine's work that there arose new and seemingly endless cultural and ecclesiastical possibilities for other historical epochs, the medieval and our own included—possibilities of which he could not then conceivably have dreamed.

An Uncharted Sea

The long-term trends that define our cultural epoch set for us the form of our major theological problems. They do not give us our symbols: the biblical and Christian traditions do that. But they do determine what we worry and think about, and how we go about that concerned reflection. These same long-term trends have set before us one more problem that must be mentioned—namely, the question of the relation of Christianity to other religions. This is by no means a new problem for Christianity; nevertheless, it appears now in a radically new way. Theologically, therefore, it represents a quite uncharted sea, one where even the major rocks, let alone the clear channels, are as yet completely unknown. This question of the relation of Christianity to other religions has been raised both at home (as noted above) and in the now close encounter of cultures in the wider world.

Certainly it has been the sociological reality of "one world" that has brought the wide variety of religions of the world into continual and intimate contact with one another, both abroad and here at home. But it has been the sharp decline of Western dominance that has recently made that contact qualitatively different. For that decline has set these religions into a situation of equality as they meet one another rather than a situation characterized by the clear dominance of one over the others. (In fact, here in the U.S. the aura of dominance, of a preponderance of illuminating and healing power, seems now to hover about the newcomers!)

Whenever religions encounter one another as equals, the sparks of theological problems—important for each—immediately shower out in all directions. If there is truth and grace in this other religion—and how can I now deny *that?*—how am I now to interpret the truth and grace I experience or hope to experience in my own? Am I to deny the latter, my own "stance" in my own faith, in order to recognize the former, the truth of the other's stance—and *thus* to have a dialogue among equals? Possibly—but then, having scuttled my own position, are we now in any sense equal? And what if my Buddhist friend does the same? Then *neither* of us represents a religious tradition, and no dialogue ensues; in fact, we have both joined a common "secular" tradition, and all we can now discuss are methods for the study of the religion of others.

Surely, then, I must continue to affirm the truth and grace in my own tradition and continue to stand *there*, if we are to speak meaningfully with one another; and yet at the same time I cannot, for the same reason, deny the truth and grace in his or her position. At that point, I am forced to try to understand *theologically* how to make sense of such a weird amalgam of an "absolute" position in my own faith with a "relative" view of it in relation to his "faith"—an amalgam that characterizes both of us in the dialogue.

As is evident, these questions raise all sorts of fundamental issues for Christian theology: about God, about "revelation," about the decisiveness of the event of Christ—and corresponding questions for members of each of the other faiths (e.g., how veridical or "absolute" in this context *is* the "higher level of consciousness" of the Buddhists?). That few know answers to these new theological issues, or even how to approach them, is obvious. But that this new situation of encounter calls for a new sort of theological discussion, and that this represents another very significant task of theology, seems to me unquestioned.

Requirements of a Risky Situation

I said at the start that I felt myself to be in a radically new situation in theology, encountering theological issues that seemed quite new and about which I felt little present clarity or as yet little real hint of an answer. And more mystifying still, while the one (the necessity of a Christian Word to a culture in mortal distress) seems to call for a sure, a clear and a well-founded Christian theology of history, the other (the necessity of dialogue with other religions) seems to relativize, though it cannot in the end dissolve, any particular religion's answer to culture's problems.

Nevertheless, these two new issues, arising as implications of the same worldwide trends, interweave and support as well as oppose or contend with each other. The ecological center of our culture's agony calls for a new view of nature—and therefore for Christians as well as secular humanists to listen carefully and receptively to the attitudes toward nature characteristic of other religious traditions. Meanwhile, the problem of a theological understanding of *history*—necessary if we in the West or those in Asia are to address either the ecological issue or the new shape of world culture—is precisely that element in our tradition for which other religions have the greatest respect and for which, on their own admission, they in turn have the greatest present need.

And, to sum this up, it is the *hermeneutical* problem with which we began which *all* modern religious traditions share in common, for which they each offer their own unique procedures, and so about which they can endlessly dialogue creatively with one another. For all of us alike face the same issue of understanding our own tradition in the light of our modern cultural and social situations—only let us, in assaying that problem, not forget the present precariousness, the moral temptations and the religious requirements of that infinitely risky modern situation!

CARL F. H. HENRY

American Evangelicals in a Turning Time

Will the world later in this century perceive Christianity as the global religion par excellence? I am now less inclined to think so than in 1970. We Christians may have to reconcile ourselves to a growing misperception that Christianity is but one among the many living religions; worse yet, we may see our commitment to it increasingly detested and persecuted. Even in the so-called free world, the educational metaview and the mass media's value ratings are already exiling Christian distinctives. Communism's vaunted world revolution, if it comes, will consign true Christians (not syncretists) to some gigantic Gulag.

Internal Weaknesses

I am even less sure of America's world leadership role. The post-Vietnam era has placed in question our nation's moral leadership, our political wisdom, our economic competence, even our military adequacy, and not least of all our national resolve and sense of fixed purpose. Leadership is God's gift to a nation, forfeiture of leadership a divine judgment upon it. While military supremacy may discourage predator powers and military weakness encourage them, national influence suspended only on military advantage is tenuous at best. Tapering all problems to politico-economic and military decisions will collapse the human spirit. America not only faces formidable foreign foes but vacillates in countering internal weaknesses that threaten to lower the flag to half-staff permanently.

I think we are now living in the very decade when God may thunder his awesome *paradidōmai* (I abandon, or I give [them] up) (Rom. 1:24 ff.) over America's professed greatness. Our massacre of a million fetuses a year; our deliberate flight from the monogamous family; our normalizing of fornication and of homosexuality and other sexual perversion; our programming of self-indulgence above social and familial concerns—all represent a quantum leap in moral deterioration, a leap more awesome than even the supposed qualitative gulf between conventional weapons and nuclear missiles. Our nation has all but tripped the worst ratings on God's Richter scale of fully deserved moral judgment.

It troubles me that some of my theological colleagues view such judgments on sexual vice as but a prudish and secondary preoccupation; they prefer, as they say, to gauge national well-being by our sensitivity to minorities and to poverty. I carry no flag for discrimination or for destitution, and readily acknowledge the importance of structural changes in society. But altered social conditions do not necessarily advance social justice. Insightful cultural concern, on the other hand, will reflect the New Testament's strong indictment of sexual infidelity and will offer a spiritual alternative to ethical emptiness.

A Strangling Humanism

When judgment falls, it will be only a matter of academic debate whether it was the disunity of professing Christians, as ecumenists think, that frustrated the emergence of "the great world church," or whether it was the doctrinal compromises of ecumenical pluralists or the short-sighted squabbling of evangelical independents that spurred the breakdown of Western technological civilization. The final denouement will reflect, no doubt, not only the spirited rebellion of an unrepentant world order and the overruling providence of God, but also both evangelical and ecumenical causal factors. In any case, Asian, African and eastern European Christians are more prepared for suffering than are Western Christians. Will the Son of Man, when he comes, find faith in our crumbling penthouses and condominiums?

It seems to me that despite its priority for sociopolitical change, organized Protestantism shows little strength for stemming the secular tide. It ineffectively confronts the strangling humanism that permeates university learning and that shortchanges generations of young people. It powerlessly contests the mass media, particularly television, whose ideal image of humanity and portrayal of life styles depict Christian claims as obscurantist and archaic. By defecting from revealed truths and fixed ethical principles, neo-Protestantism weakens its mediating proposals; to compensate for a lack of intellectual and moral suasion it readily aspires to political power. The conflicting claims of the Mediator and the secular media, of the Archon and of academe, seem to me to represent decisive alternatives in the battle for public perception of the right and the good throughout the '80s.

We should commend the electronic church for its venturesome outreach to parched multitudes thirsting for what activists readily overlook in their assault on social structures—namely, a personal faith. But much television religion is too experience-centered, too doctrinally thin, to provide an adequate alternative to modern religious and moral confusion. Yet critics of the charismatic movement all too easily forget that the spiritually reborn often naïvely accept all the marginal trappings attaching to their first discovery of the crucified and risen Redeemer. It is true, nonetheless, that charismatic religion may indeed become a catchall that shelters rival spiritual authorities and requires no specifically Christian profession whatever.

A Cognitive Vacuum

The dull theological edge of American Christianity desperately needs sharpening. No literate society can afford to postpone cognitive considerations. Why Christ and not Buddha? Why Christianity and not Hare Krishna? Why biblical theism and not process philosophy? Why the gospel and not amphetamines? Half-generation novelties in theology, I am persuaded, offer no adequate reply.

Yo-yo theology—that is, perpetually restructured belief—is less my forte than Yahweh theology, the "faith once-for-all delivered." Neither an evening with Bultmann in a Wiesbaden *Weinhaus* nor dinner with Tillich when he gave the Gifford Lectures in Aberdeen, nor that long walk with Brunner through the streets of Zurich, nor periodic chats with Barth in his Basel home shook my conviction that scriptural theism holds a logic absent from recent modern theology. In the writings of the bright-flashing contemporary stars, including the more angry apostles of revolution theology, I find an unfilled cognitive vacuum, one that leaves the mind merely a mood ahead of those skeptical critics intent on killing the Almighty.

It was not, to be sure, the logic of Christian theism that specially spurred me to Christian decision as a young newspaper reporter and editor, although any conviction of its illogic would have turned me away. Nor had I come to Christ, as have many others, by family inheritance or by churchly absorption. What piqued my curiosity was the inviting prospect, dangled by a university graduate, of what Jesus Christ can do for one who fully trusts him. Across the years I learned, however, that although Jesus Christ holds fast his own, one cannot confidently hold fast what Christ does unless one also embraces truth along with mercy and righteousness. The credibility of the Judeo-Christian revelation is what precludes reducing Christ to simply one option among many.

A decade ago I thought that late 20th century America might be on the move, however hesitantly, toward a theological renaissance. Even if Barth, Bultmann and Tillich, beyond their notable impact on seminaries, had little influence on the temper of the universities and on the mood of the churches, might not evangelical Christianity, I wondered, break out of its evangelistic halter? Might not evangelicals who were beginning to wrestle with sociopolitical concerns also take theology more seriously?

At present I see too little prospect of that. Instead of emphasizing the universal truth-claim exerted by the Bible upon the mind and conscience of all humankind, one spokesperson after another fulminates against evangelical "rationalism" and retreats to personal commitment. The notion of comprehensive culture-conditioning is met concessively rather than critically. The prevalent rejection of an objectively authoritative Scripture is countered by irresponsible polemic; instead of finding a communist under every bed it charts an enemy list within every evangelical enterprise. Where is the comprehensive sense of a mighty armory of revealed truth that calls to council the whole arena of modern learning?

Equating Justice with Socialism

Meanwhile, many ecumenically oriented seminaries, titillated by what is novel, and seemingly unable to learn from history, baptize anything revolutionary as the wave of the future. Neo-Protestant giants of the recent past, all but forgotten on much ecumenical turf, are now getting a more deferential, if belated, hearing on concessive evangelical campuses. Nonevangelicals are turning anew to the social gospel which equates biblical justice with socialism, sometimes reconstituting it as a "theology of hope" promoted by protest and pressure, and seeking allies among evangelical *Sojourners*. They project salvific universalism with new passion, emphasize ethical preaching more than theological consensus, reach for hermeneutical methods that confer biblical legitimacy on culture-oriented options; they consider doctrinal pluralism an enrichment that might foster a revival of COCU and perchance some link with Roman Catholicism.

All this adds up, as I see it, to little more than "whistling in the dark." The penetrating question that hangs over the ecumenical churches is not what form their global union might take, but whether denominations losing as many as a million members a year or making few adult converts will survive the 20th century.

I remain unpersuaded that any theological movement can dramatically affect the course of the world while its own leaders undermine the integrity of its charter documents, or while its spokespersons domestically exhaust all their energies in internal defense of those documents. The Bible stands impressively unshaken by the fury of destructive critics, while the nonbelieving world, itself marked for destruction, urgently needs to hear its singular message of salvation.

Lost Opportunities

While 40 million evangelical Protestants in the United States have immense resources to implement this Christian world task, they too often fritter away opportunities for joint endeavor, or expect to achieve every goal through too few and too limited programs. The besetting weakness of evangelicals is their lack of a comprehensive and coordinated strategy that welds intellectual, evangelistic and ethical resources into effective cooperation. This lack condemns them to a mainly reactionary course and a commentary role on the initiatives of nonevangelicals. The significant proportion of evangelicals within the ecumenically organized denominations has not—even if some still hope to do so—countered the drift to theological pluralism, to missionary and evangelistic retrenchment, to social-action priorities, to debatable hierarchical commitments that some aroused church members and many of the clergy resent.

What do the well-attended evangelical churches portend for the future? What will be the impact of their burgeoning colleges marked by life-changing vitality and moral earnestness? What of the vocal church memberships that now increasingly demand a voice in public affairs?

During the 1960s I somewhat romanced the possibility that a vast evangelical alliance might arise in the United States to coordinate effectively a national impact in evangelism, education, publication and sociopolitical action. Such an alliance is not the same thing as a new denomination. Quite apart from the question of its desirability, the remote possibility of such a national evangelical alliance was both shaped and lost, it seems to me, by evangelist Billy Graham. Penetrating the so-called mainline denominations with an evangelical rallying point, the Graham crusades reached far beyond the orbit of the National Association of Evangelicals. As the tide of enthusiasm for pluralistic ecumenism began to ebb, the prospect emerged for a mighty evangelical movement that transcended secondary denominational distinctions; it held in promise a transdenominational link involving Southern Baptists, the National Association of Evangelicals, Missouri Synod Lutherans, perhaps some associates of the American Council of Churches, and large numbers of disaffected evangelicals in ecumenically affiliated churches whom the NAE seemed unable to attract. *Christianity Today* became during my editorship (1956–68) an intellectual fulcrum for these overlapping evangelical concerns.

Graham is himself a Southern Baptist. Although he had the personal magnetism to rally and garner an umbrella alliance, he hesitated to do so. For his crusades he sought the fullest possible ecumenical backing, even if it often came grudgingly. To call for an evangelical countermovement that might penetrate ecumenical ranks would have eroded ecumenical support for the crusades. Graham was simultaneously under NAE pressures to extend that organization's paraecumenical opportunities. By the early 1970s the prospect of a massive evangelical alliance seemed annually more remote, and by mid-decade it was gone.

Obstacles arose not simply because of denominational differences but also because of rival goals. Instead of uniting on something feasible, evangelicals too often backed away from the best option only to support nothing.

Prospects for a national evangelical university to be located in the suburban New York area faltered in the '60s when some conferees pushed for a new Presbyterian seminary, others for a Bible college, still others for reinforcement of Wheaton as an already existing liberal arts college. Graham's colleagues held that the evangelist should be personally rewarded with the presidency because of his unique access to necessary sources of endowment, but then opposed a university since administrative responsibilities would curtail evangelistic priorities.

New Movements to the Fore

In the '70s *Christianity Today* appealed more to lay readers and moved noticeably toward evangelical independency. The magazine gave only token support to Key '73, whose stimulus had come from an earlier editorial ("Somehow Let's Get Together"). It viewed evangelical social action with high reservation, although the editor publicly indicated support of Nixon's candidacy. Then, at the very time national newsmagazines spoke of "the year of the evangelical," *Christianity Today* turned more inward than outward by channeling all theological issues into the inerrancy debate. The present staff strives to redress these misjudgments.

Many evangelical subgroups representing special interests stepped into this vacuum of missed evangelical opportunity. Magazines like *Sojourners*, the *Other Side* and the *Reformed Journal* took antiestablishment positions; divergent Calvinistic and Arminian groups sought a revitalized influence; evangelical social-action groups arose with varying emphases. Additional movements came to the fore: World Vision's spectacular global ministry of evangelical humanitarianism; the charismatic phenomenon; the flourishing electronic church; the new core of Roman Catholic evangelicals; the Fuller Theological Seminary's pro-ecumenical stance and alignment with critical views of the Bible; ecumenical alliances by left-wing evangelicals; politically right-wing groups like Moral Majority.

Establishment evangelicalism was reinforced by the Billy Graham Center's location at Wheaton College, by *Christianity Today's* removal from Washington, D.C., to Chicago suburbs where evangelical independency has deep roots, and by formation of the International Council on Biblical Inerrancy.

Numerous crosscurrents now vex almost every effort at comprehensive evangelical liaison. At present no single leader or agency has the respect, magnetism or platform to summon all divergent elements to conference. Evangelical differences increasingly pose an identity crisis.

Intellectual Awakening

For all that, the strength of evangelical Christianity lies in its confident vision of the supernatural, its emphasis on revealed truths and divine commandments, its evangelistic energy and life-transforming power. That strength is all the more evident at a time when the most prestigious universities, the most influential media, and even many theologians lack any sure grip on these realities. Yet American evangelicalism is not as strong as its proponents think; it appears stronger than it is because of the disarray of ecumenical and of Catholic Christianity, as well as the ethical relativity and personal meaninglessness of secular life.

Noteworthy signs of evangelical intellectual awakening are in the wind, however. Within the American Philosophical Association, a Society of Christian Philosophers has emerged with impressive evangelical participation. Hundreds of evangelical scholars are completing specialized doctorates to prepare for teaching careers. The Institute for Advanced Christian Studies is sponsoring an important series of college textbooks on Christianity and modern intellectual concerns. Tens of thousands of university students have made evangelical commitments despite the counterthrust of radically secular humanism. From these young intellectuals will come a literate clergy and qualified academics to help realign liberal-arts learning in a quest for the whole truth.

Not only has Protestant ecumenism exerted little theistic impact upon the academic and media worlds, but its insistent demand for altered social structures has achieved few decisive changes. Many Christians find both major political parties objectionably laden with humanist perspectives.

As the author of *The Uneasy Conscience of Modern Fundamentalism* (1947), I can only welcome the evangelical return to public involvement. Even if one regrets the neglect or absence of a comprehensive agenda and the pursuit, instead, of single-issue and single-candidate concerns, and regrets even more the lack of a governing political philosophy, the times and issues are such that open debate must be welcomed on as broad a platform as possible.

My mind-shifts during the past decade include a deepening conviction that justice is not self-defining and that divergent definitions of justice now plunge the modern world anew into a "struggle between the gods." I am convinced that only with great agony, and in view of the shoddy track record of recreant predatory powers, should the nation commit itself to ever more staggering military expenditures. Inflation may now be irreversible, a specter spawned by political leaders whom we entrusted to watch the storehouse. It may be also that Western middle-class affluence will soon be recognized not as the universal ideal but as a remarkable exception in human history, one bearing great stewardship opportunities and responsibilities for worldwide extension of the gospel and for helping the underprivileged to help themselves.

Ten years ago I put less emphasis on the requisite indictment of unjust structures. I remain less confident than social activists that any of us will achieve ideal alternatives, or even better structures. History beset by human perversity will find ideal alternatives only when the Messiah ushers in the new heaven and new earth. We must nonetheless try, guarding all the while against prejudicial and propagandistic notions of what is "better." To truncate the Christian mission simply to the changing of social structures profoundly misunderstands the biblical view of human nature and divine redemption. Yet we also truncate the gospel if we limit or circumvent the expectation that divine deliverance will extend "far as the curse is found."

Christ's sinless life and his resurrection as the Crucified One carry assurance of his victory over all sin's powers, including injustice and exploitation. To proclaim the criteria by which the Coming King will judge persons and nations, to exemplify those standards in the church as the new society, and to work for their recognition by the world—these are irreducible aspects of the Christian summons to the forgiveness of sins and new life, and to the lordship of the risen and returning King.

Revelation and Culture

The key intellectual issue for the '80s, as I see it, will still be the persistent problem of authority. It will concern especially the problem of hermeneutics, and centrally the question of revelation and culture. Those who argue that revelation is enculturated will be unable to exempt their own pontifications. Christianity's true immortals will insist that God addresses the truth of revelation objectively to all humans of whatever diverse cultures.

God, who has an eye on the poor, and perhaps specially on us 20th century theologians, in his infinite wisdom inscribed the Decalogue on tablets of stone (Deut. 4:13, 10:4) and spoke (Num. 22:28 ff.) by Balaam's ass. God's spokesmen may be confused, but the ass knows his master's manger (Isa. 1:3); stones no less than scrolls will praise God's transcendent revelation (Luke 19:40) when Christ's professing disciples are tongue-tied.

II

Christian Theology
in a Time of
Religious Pluralism

JOHN MBITI

The Encounter of Christian Faith and African Religion

In my reflections on "How My Mind Has Changed" in the course of the past decade, I wish to apply "change of mind" to mean theological growth, and not necessarily a rejection of or turnaround from ideas that I may have held ten years ago. Indeed, ten years ago I had no significant theological position. I was like a snail shyly peeping out of its house after a heavy thunderstorm.

". . . In Africa, God Is Not Dead"

I completed my doctoral studies at the University of Cambridge in 1963, the year that *Honest to God*, by John A. T. Robinson, came out. That book was followed by a flurry of literature on the so-called "death of God" theology (if "theology" it was, for I would call it "atheology"). Following a period of parish work in England, I went to teach at Makerere University, Uganda, where I remained for ten years, until 1974. One read *Honest to God* and a variety of other works in an effort to understand the hot debate then raging in Europe and America. Some people tried to involve Africa in the debate. But to the disappointment of those theological exporters, this fish was not attracted by the bait. A prominent European New Testament professor visited Makerere University and interviewed me on what I thought about the "death of God" discussion. I simply and honestly answered him that "for us in Africa, God is not dead." That finished the interview. On returning home, the learned professor wrote an article using my brief answer as his title.

At Makerere University I taught New Testament, African religion and other courses. Since I myself had never heard any lectures on African religion, I set out to do research on the subject in order to teach the course adequately. The first and most intriguing topic that immediately engaged my attention was the thinking of African peoples about God. So I read on and on, and conducted field research to learn more and more. My findings were used in teaching, but eventually I put them together in a book, *Concepts of God in Africa*, published by the British publisher SPCK (1970). The book comprised ideas that I had gathered from 300 African peoples ("tribes"—a term that today is sometimes used in derogatory ways). The previous year I had published *African Religions and Philosophy* (Doubleday, 1969).

Some individuals have criticized these books—and no book is perfect. But whatever the shortcomings of these and my other publications, the materials that went into these two have raised extremely important issues for me that have continued to engage my reflection. At many points I see intriguing parallels between the biblical record and African religiosity. In particular, the concepts about God provide one area of great commonality. There are also other parallels in social, political and cultural areas, just as there are some significant differences. In one case the thinking and experience of the people produced a written record of God's dealings with the Jewish people in particular. In the other case no such written record exists. But God's dealings with the African people are recorded, nevertheless, in living form—oral communication, rituals, symbols, ceremonies, community faith. "For us in Africa, God is not dead"—and that applies whether or not there is a written record of his relations with and concern for people.

A God Already Known

Since the Bible tells me that God is the creator of all things, his activities in the world must clearly go beyond what is recorded in the Bible. He must have been active among African peoples as he was among the Jewish people. Did he then reveal himself *only* in the line of Abraham, Isaac, Jacob, Moses, Samuel and other personalities of the Bible? Didn't our Lord let it be clearly known that "before Abraham was I am" (John 8:58)? Then was he not there in other times and in such places as Mount Fuji and Mount Kenya, as well as Mount Sinai? The decisive word here is "only." The more I peeped into African religious insights about God, the more I felt utterly unable to use the word "only" in this case. In its place there emerged the word "also." This was an extremely liberating word in my theological thinking. With it, one began to explore afresh the realm of God's revelation and other treasures of our faith. I find the traditional Western distinction between "special revelation" and "general revelation" to be inadequate and unfreeing. This is not a biblical distinction. If they are two wavelengths, they make sense only when they move toward a convergence. When this happens, then a passage such as Hebrews 1:1–3 rolls down like mighty waters, full of exciting possibilities of theological reflection.

The God described in the Bible is none other than the God who is already known in the framework of our traditional African religiosity. The missionaries who introduced the gospel to Africa in the past 200 years did not bring God to our continent. Instead, God brought *them*. They proclaimed the name of Jesus Christ. But they used the names of the God who was and is already known by African peoples—such as Mungu, Mulungu, Katonda, Ngai, Olodumare, Asis, Ruwa, Ruhanga, Jok, Modimo, Unkulunkulu and thousands more. These were not empty names. They were names of one and the same God, the creator of the world, the father of our Lord Jesus Christ. One African theologian, Gabriel Setiloane, has even argued that the concept of God which the missionaries presented to the Sotho-Tswana peoples was a devaluation of the traditional currency of Modimo (God) among the Sotho-Tswana.

No doubt there still remain much research and reflection to be done in order to work out a consistent theological understanding of the issues entailed here. But the basic truth seems to be that God's revelation is not confined to the biblical record. One important task, then, is to see the nature, the method and the implications of God's revelation among African peoples, in the light of the biblical record of the same revelation.

Revelation is given not in a vacuum but within particular historical experiences and reflections. When we identify the God of the Bible as the same God who is known through African religion (whatever its limitations), we must also take it that God has had a historical relationship with African peoples. God is not insensitive to the history of peoples other than Israel. Their history has a theological meaning. My interpretation of Israel's history demands a new look at the history of African peoples, among whom this same God of Abraham, Isaac and Jacob has indeed been at work. In this case, so-called "salvation history" must widen its outreach in order to embrace the horizons of other peoples' histories. I am not a historian, and I have not done careful thinking in this direction. But I feel that the issue of looking at African history in light of the biblical understanding of history is clearly called for.

A Massive Expansion

My research into and teaching of African religion has led to another important area of development. In Kenya I grew up in home, school and church milieus which held that the African religious and cultural background was demonic and anti-Christian. In this overpowering environment, one simply accepted this stand and looked at the world from its perspectives. Later, my theological studies in America and England did not challenge this position, since that was not a living issue for my professors and fellow students. But upon my return to work in Africa, and upon careful study of the religious background of our people, there emerged gradually the demand to examine this issue and to form my own judgment.

The statistical expansion of the Christian faith in Africa in this century is one of the considerations that led me back to the issue of its relation with African religion. In 1900 there were an estimated 9 million Christians (accounting for about 7 per cent of the population of Africa). This number has since grown rapidly, to the point that in 1980 there were estimated to be 200 million Christians (or about 45 per cent of the population). This massive expansion within such a short time is unprecedented in the history of Christianity. What factors are responsible for it?

We can list some obvious and often publicized factors. They include the work of missionaries (of whom there are about 40,000 today, without counting their family members); the work of African Christians in evangelism and pastoral care (their numbers are infinitely greater than those of overseas missionaries, and include men, women and children, both lay and ordained); the role of Christian schools; the translation and distribution of the Bible (which is now available in full or in part in nearly 600 of Africa's 1,000 languages); and the ending of the colonial era during the decades 1960–1980. But I have discovered that there is also the fundamental factor of African religion, without which this phenomenal expansion of Christianity would not be a reality. Of course, behind all these factors is the Holy Spirit working through them.

There is not space here to argue the case for the role played by African religion in the establishment of the Christian faith in Africa. We have already noted that the overseas missionaries did not bring God to Africa. God was not a stranger to African peoples. Spiritual activities like prayer, thanksgiving, and the making of sacrifices were well-established facts of life for the existence and continuation of the community.

The Church in the African Scene

It is in this complex of religiosity that the preaching of the gospel makes sense; it is this preparedness that has undergirded the spreading of the gospel like wildfire among African societies which had hitherto followed and practiced traditional religion. Consequently, people are discovering that the biblical faith is not harmful to their religious sensibilities. This is, obviously, a general statement, one which needs detailed elaboration. But in practical terms, there is a Christian Yes to African religiosity. It may be, and needs to be, a qualified and critical Yes. But it is nevertheless a working Yes and one that demands theological understanding. A close geographical correlation exists between the location of African religion and the rapid expansion of the Christian faith. This is not an empty coincidence. It is the southern two-thirds of Africa (including Madagascar) which we can rightly call Christian Africa, as the northern one-third is Muslim Africa.

This rapid spreading of the Christian faith where people have been predominantly followers of African religion provokes interesting questions. That which had been seen as the enemy of the gospel turns out (to me) to be indeed a very welcoming friend. African religion has equipped people to listen to the gospel, to discover meaningful passages in the Bible, and to avoid unhealthy religious conflict.

Theological development in Africa must inevitably grow within this religious setting. For this reason, some African theologians take African religiosity to be one of the sources of theological reflection (besides the Bible, Christian heritage, etc.). A conference of mainly African theologians, held in Ghana in December 1977, said in its final communiqué: "The God of history speaks to all peoples in particular ways. In Africa the traditional religions are a major source for the study of the African experience of God. The beliefs and practices of the traditional religions in Africa can enrich Christian theology and spirituality." These statements await further exploration by African theologians. Currently I am about to complete a book on this question of the encounter between the biblical faith and African religion.

The church is composed largely of people who come out of the African religious background. Their culture, history, world views and spiritual aspirations cannot be taken away from them. These impinge upon their daily life and experience of the Christian faith. So the church which exists on the African scene bears the marks of its people's backgrounds.

No viable theology can grow in Africa without addressing itself to the interreligious phenomenon at work there. I feel deeply the value of biblical studies in this exercise, and the contribution of biblical insights in this development.

The Quest for Christian Unity

I have concentrated these comments on the role of African background in my theological reflection. There are other areas of exploration in which I continue to be engaged. There is no room to describe them, and I can mention only two or three of them briefly. My doctoral studies in New Testament eschatology led me also to the field of Christology. I want to reflect and write on this topic, but somehow it makes me feel frightened. I want to make a pilgrimage into Christ. I want to walk with Jesus of Nazareth on the shores of Lake Galilee and the hillsides of Judea, through the gates of Jerusalem. I want to see his healing hand, to hear his word that exorcises evil spirits.

For six years I worked with the World Council of Churches in Geneva. That experience gave me a face-to-face encounter with the ecumenical movement and left a lasting mark on me. It sensitized my thinking in many areas, one of these being the quest for Christian unity. I have seen the quest more sharply. I cannot claim that I have witnessed much progress in that quest at the organizational level, but perhaps I had expected too much. The council made me aware, perhaps even frightfully so, of the problems of our world. The council's programs in response to these problems are impressive. They constitute an important channel of the church's prophetic witness today. The WCC's very existence as a council of churches is a living hope. But it has been a sorrowful disappointment to me to experience the fact that some individuals who exercise great power in the council are not angels: they sometimes practice the exact contrary of those values and goals to which the council is committed. Nevertheless, I am convinced that the World Council of Churches is a great witness of the Christian response to the prayer of our Lord that we may all be one. And this witness deserves one's support through service and prayer.

A Tilting from North to South

The concept of the church as the body of Christ in the whole world is another growing development for me. I have been greatly enriched by working at the Ecumenical Institute at Bossey, 1974–1980. It is here that I have discovered the church in Burma, in the Pacific islands, the house church in China, the basic Christian communities in Latin America, the struggling church in South Africa, plus countless other endeavors of Christians all over the world. I have met here the church not only in its geographical outreach but also in its historical roots—seeing, for example, the rich traditions of the Orthodox Church, the universality of the Roman Catholic Church (even though it is based in the Vatican), the reconciling positioning of the Anglican Communion, the dynamic vitality of African independent churches, and so on. I have received much in a short period. It will keep me chewing for a long time, and it will most certainly feed my theological development.

I am very excited, for example, by the estimate that in 1987 there will be a statistical balance of Christian population between the north (Europe, Soviet Union and America) and the south (Latin America, Africa, Asia and Oceania). After that date there will be more Christians in the south than in the north. This statistical tilting of Christendom from the north to the south, after 2,000 years, holds tremendous prospects and challenges. Its consequences for theological and ecclesiological developments are yet to be faced. They will certainly be overwhelming, and I feel very excited about them.

The theological horizon continues to expand. I am tantalized by the fact that my vision cannot cope with that horizon. But I am grateful for that one step I may be taking under the light of this vision. So, "Lord, help Thou my unbelief!" Amen.

JOHN HICK

Pluralism and the Reality of the Transcendent

The past decade has been to me extremely stimulating and challenging as the horizon of problems in my field has expanded. Ten or 12 years ago I was concerned with philosophical and theological questions solely as they arose within the context of Christian belief. Now—late in the day in comparison with many others—I have become concerned with these and other questions in a wider intercultural and interreligious context. It now seems more important, and more illuminating, to study the multifarious relationships of humankind as a whole to the divine than to study, as an isolated phenomenon, only that particular form of faith within which I happen to be.

A Context of Pluralism

Before looking at the changed morphology of problems within the larger context, let me indicate briefly my own personal route to this new vantage point. It is one more exemplification of the familiar fact that the shape of one's life and the color of one's outlook are formed largely by unpredictable contingencies. Having taught very happily for ten years in the United States (at Cornell University and Princeton Theological Seminary), I felt drawn to return with my family to England, and went to a lectureship in the philosophy of religion at Cambridge University in a very active and stimulating period of its faculty of divinity. But in England there is usually only one chair (or, in American terms, full professorship) in a given subject in each university; the total of such positions in the philosophy of religion in the whole country is less than a dozen.

And so, moved by ordinary professional considerations, I applied for and was appointed, in 1967, to the next philosophy of religion chair to become vacant—the one at the University of Birmingham, located in a city about which I then knew little. Birmingham had become, in the years since World War II, a multiracial, multicultural and multifaith city, about a tenth of its 1 million inhabitants being immigrants or the children of immigrants from the Indian subcontinent and the Caribbean islands. The latter are black Christians (or post-Christians), while the former are Muslims, Sikhs and Hindus. Birmingham also has a long-established Jewish community, and there are in addition a small number of Buddhists. Thus the religious traditions of both East and West, and indeed all the major world faiths, are represented in the city.

I was quickly drawn into various activities in response to the practical problems of Birmingham's pluralism, and thus into contact with the black community and with the various non-Christian religious groups. Occasionally attending worship in mosque and synagogue, temple and gurdwara, I came to see as evident that essentially the same activity takes place in them as in a Christian church: human beings meet, within the framework of a particular religious culture, to open their spirits to a higher reality which is regarded both as being the source of all their good and as making a total claim upon the living of their lives. Contact with these non-Christian worshiping communities led me to read about the world religions more seriously than I had done before, and to spend three study leaves (amounting together to nearly a year) in Hindu India and Buddhist Sri Lanka.

In the course of all this it has become abundantly clear to me that, at its best, each of the great world faiths constitutes a perception of and a response to the ultimate divine reality which they all in their different ways affirm; and also that within each there are to be found true saints through whom the Transcendent shines within the fabric of our human life. It is also clear that at its worst each religion sanctifies the cruelty, ignorance, sloth, selfishness and violent propensities of our human species. If we compare one religion at its best with another at its worst, we readily establish the superiority of the former. But considering them as totalities we can only acknowledge that within each the process of salvation/liberation/human-perfecting can and does take place, although we cannot quantify its incidence within the different traditions.

The Reality of the Eternal One

This view of humankind's religious life is sometimes called relativism, but is, I think, more appropriately called pluralism. For in contrast to the confessional affirmation that there is only one realm of genuine salvation and true awareness of the divine, namely one's own, this view affirms a plurality of such realms. Pluralism involves, of course, as many and as great philosophical and religious problems as does confessionalism; but they are different problems, and it is with some of this different set of problems that I have been engaged in recent years in my books *God and the Universe of Faiths, Death and Eternal Life* and *God Has Many Names.*

Let us call the ultimate object of religious worship, experience and contemplation "the Eternal One"—a phrase which draws upon associations both with "the mystical One without a second" of the Upanishads and "the Holy One" of the biblical and other theistic faiths. The basic problem in the philosophy of religion is that of the reality of the Eternal One—in traditional Western thought, of the existence of God. There is here a continuity between the concerns of confessionalism and those of pluralism. In either case the basic issue is that of the reality of the Transcendent. And so the opposition in which I engaged in the previous decade against noncognitive analyses of religious language—for example, that drawn from the later work of Wittgenstein—has continued during the past ten years.

Believing that such analyses are untrue to the actual intention of religious-language users, I still want to consider and evaluate the grounds on which human beings believe in a transcendent reality in which being and value are one. Impressive attempts have been made to show that the affirmation of such a reality is a necessity for rational thought. Two such attempts, the ontological and cosmological proofs, have had important revivals in recent years. The arguments involved are complex and fascinating, and I have spent some time with them in *The Many-Faced Argument* (in collaboration with the late Arthur McGill of Harvard) and *Arguments for the Existence of God.*

But the "bottom line" can, I believe, be only that none of the traditional theistic arguments finally succeeds. However, it must surely be significant that none of the great world religions was in fact launched by philosophical arguments. Such reasonings were developed later in the course of communicating or defending what was already believed on other grounds. Nor can those other grounds be reduced to belief on the authority of someone else, some great spiritual leader; rather, they must be the grounds on which such spiritual leaders themselves believed. And these grounds are in the area of religious experience. The conviction of the reality of the Transcendent, when it is based in religious experience, is an acknowledgment of a presence or a power which impinges upon someone's consciousness, whether gently or traumatically, so that to deny it would be an act of spiritual suicide.

Given such firsthand awareness of the divine, the appropriate philosophical apologetic is a defense of the rationality of trusting and living on the basis of compelling experience of this kind. Without attempting to develop it here, I believe that such an apologetic is possible. In Christian terms, its conclusion is that one who experiences his or her life, in greater or lesser degree, as being lived in the presence of God, as made known to us by Jesus, is rationally entitled to believe in the reality of that God, and to proceed to live accordingly. But if such an argument holds for the Christian experience of the divine, it must also hold for the Jewish, the Muslim, the Hindu, the Buddhist experiences. One must follow the Golden Rule and grant to religious experience within the other great traditions the same presumption of cognitive veridicality that one quite properly claims for one's own.

Images of God

It is at this point that we meet the problem of the very different and apparently conflicting reports of the Divine coming from the different religious traditions. Can the Eternal One be at once the Adonai of Judaism, the Father of Jesus Christ, the Allah of Islam, the Krishna and the Shiva of theistic Hinduism, the Brahman of advaitic Hinduism, the Dharmakaya or the Sunyata of Mahayana Buddhism, and the Nirvana of Theravada Buddhism? If we presume the basically cognitive character of religious experience within the great traditions, we shall, I believe, be led to draw a distinction between, on the one hand, the Eternal One in itself, as the infinite Reality which exceeds the scope of human thought, language and experience, and, on the other hand, the Eternal One as experienced, thought and expressed by finite human creatures.

We shall then study the differences between our human ways of experiencing and thinking the divine. For, in St. Thomas's dictum, "The thing known is in the knower according to the mode of the knower" (*Summa Theologica*, II/II, Q.1, art. 2); and in religion there seem to be many communities of knowers with different though overlapping modes of cognition. Human experience is structured by concepts, and it would seem that one or the other of two basic concepts provides the framework of religious experience. One, which presides over the theistic forms of religion, is the concept of God or of the Eternal One as personal. The other, which presides over the nontheistic forms of religion, is the concept of the Absolute or of the Eternal One as nonpersonal. (It should, incidentally, be noted that both forms of religious awareness appear within each of the great world traditions, though in different modes and proportions.)

But these very general categorical concepts do not as such form the actual experience of individuals and communities. These ideas take more concrete or particular forms as specific images or "pictures" of God, or as specific concepts of the Absolute. Thus the general idea of deity has been concretized in Hebrew experience in the image of Yahweh as a personal being who exists in interaction with the Jewish people. He is a part of their history and they are a part of his. But Yahweh is different from, say, Krishna, who is a distinctively Hindu *persona* of the Eternal One in relation to the Vaishnavite community of India. Again, the basic concept of the Absolute is particularized in different ways within the different nontheistic traditions.

This fact is, however, not readily accepted within those traditions. Their customary claim is that in the mystical state of perfect enlightenment there is a direct awareness of reality itself, undistorted by our human cognitive machinery with its variety of images of a personal deity. But in fact the different methods of meditation, the different scriptures feeding the spirit, the different philosophies and sustaining communities combine in the major Eastern traditions to produce different experiences of the ultimate reality. Thus the distinctive Zen experience is characteristically different from, for example, the distinctive advaitic experience. Here also, then, it seems that "the thing known is in the knower according to the mode of the knower."

This kind of attempt to find a global, or multifaith, epistemology of religion generates its own further questions. For example, it is obvious in principle that some perceptions of the Eternal One may be more accurate and some responses more adequate than others; and indeed, when we take account not only of the great world faiths but also of primitive religion and of the innumerable smaller, and in some cases eccentric, or repulsive, horrible and destructive religious movements of the past and the present, it is clear that we do in fact apply moral and other criteria in our reactions to them. What, then, are the proper criteria for judgment in this area? Again, what account is to be given of the nonreligious ideologies, particularly Marxism, by which so many live today? There is thus a plentiful agenda of problems for the religious pluralist.

Pluralism and Christianity

But let me now turn to the effects which a pluralist view of religion has upon one's understanding of and relationship to one's own tradition. However imperfectly (and in fact very imperfectly) this is reflected in my own life, I feel irrevocably challenged and claimed by the impact of the life and teaching of Jesus; and to be thus decisively influenced by him is, I suppose, the basic definition of a Christian. How then is my Christian faith changed by acceptance of the salvific character of the other world religions?

The older theological tradition of Christianity does not readily permit religious pluralism. For at its center is the conviction that Jesus of Nazareth was God—the Second Person of a Divine Trinity living a human life. It follows from this that Christianity, and Christianity alone, was founded by God in person on the only occasion on which he has ever become incarnate in this world, so that Christianity has a unique status as the way of salvation provided and appointed by God himself.

If this claim is to have real substance and effect, it follows that the salvation thus made possible within Christianity cannot also be possible outside it. This conclusion was drawn with impeccable logic in the Roman dogma *Extra ecclesiam nulla salus* ("Outside the church, no salvation"), and in its 19th century Protestant missionary equivalent, "Outside Christianity, no salvation." But in the light of our accumulated knowledge of the other great world faiths, this conclusion has become unacceptable to all except a minority of dogmatic diehards. For it conflicts with our concept of God, which we have received from Jesus, as the loving heavenly Father of *all* humankind; could such a Being have restricted the possibility of salvation to those who happen to have been born in certain countries in certain periods of history?

But perhaps salvation is not the issue? Perhaps salvation is taking place not only within Christianity but also outside it, while the unique Christian gospel is that God became man in Jesus to make this possible? The doctrine of atonement thus becomes central. This suggestion appeals to some as a means of acknowledging God's saving work throughout humankind while retaining the dogma of the unique centrality of Christ as the only savior of the world. But in so doing it sacrifices the substance of the older position. For the nerve of the old dogma was the imperative that it generated to convert all to faith in Jesus as their Lord and Savior: "No one comes to the Father, but by me" and "There is salvation in no one else, for there is no other name under heaven given among men whereby we must be saved." That nerve is cut when we acknowledge the other great world religions as being also areas of divine salvation.

The other kind of attempt to "have it both ways," exemplified by Karl Rahner's picture of devout persons of other faiths as "anonymous Christians," is too manifestly an ad hoc contrivance to satisfy many. For it is as easy, and as arbitrary, to label devout Christians as anonymous Muslims, or anonymous Hindus, as to label devout Hindus or Muslims as anonymous Christians.

Divine Incarnation as Metaphor

Finding such responses inadequate, I believe it is necessary to look again at the traditional interpretation of Jesus as God incarnate. Such a reconsideration is in any case required today by the realization that the historical Jesus almost certainly did not in fact teach that he was in any sense God; and also by the fact that Christian thought has not yet, despite centuries of learned attempts, been able to give any intelligible content to the idea that a finite human being, genuinely a part of our human race, was also the infinite, eternal, omnipotent, omniscient Creator of everything other than himself.

The proper conclusion to draw, as it seems to me, is that the idea of divine incarnation is a metaphorical (or in technical theological language, mythological) idea. When a truth or a value is lived out in a human life, it is a natural metaphor to speak of its being incarnated in that life. Jesus lived in full openness to God, responsive to the divine will, transparent to the divine purpose, so that he lived out the divine agape within human history. This was not a matter of his being of the same substance as God the Father, or of his having two complete natures, one human and the other divine. Agape is incarnated in human life whenever someone acts in selfless love—and this occurred in the life of Jesus to a startling and epoch-making degree. Whether he incarnated self-giving love more than anyone else who has ever lived, we cannot know. But we do know that his actual historical influence has been unique in its extent.

This kind of reinterpretation of the idea of divine incarnation is, in different forms, fairly widespread today (more so, I think, in the United States than in Britain) and provides, so it seems to me, a basis for a form of Christianity which can be part of the religiously plural world of today and tomorrow.

PAUL M. VAN BUREN

Probing the Jewish-Christian Reality

In my last conversation with Karl Barth, in 1961—a conversation that was for both of us in some ways painful—I asked him what he expected of his former students, seeing that he was so dissatisfied with what I was then doing (i.e., developing what was to be *The Secular Meaning of the Gospel*). Barth's answer was that every page of his *Dogmatics* was in need of improvement and that we should set to work to make it better. I took him to mean that we should be devoting ourselves to writing footnotes on his work. Instead, I took another path which led to some dozen years of working in analytic philosophy of religion, and that was where I was when the '70s began.

By the end of the decade, however, I was at work at the task that Barth had asked of me, not as I then heard it, but as I now hear it. The dogmatic or systematic theological work of the church, of which Barth's *Church Dogmatics* is a distinguished crown, is indeed in need of serious correction on every page, and with the years that remain, I mean to continue the task of trying to improve it.

Administrative Tasks

My change of mind in moving from the philosophy of religion to the task of systematic theology came roughly in the middle of the decade. The first third of the decade saw my last efforts at unsnarling the puzzles of religion, taken as puzzles of language. With *The Edges of Language* (1972) I had reached the limits of what I could do to understand religion with the help of the work of Ludwig Wittgenstein, and I was not impressed with the results. I was not impressed with the results which others had come up with either. Some were cleverer than others, but none of them seemed to make much of a difference. Philosophers in general—and so also philosophers of religion—were simply writing for each other, and their results seemed to me to have little to do with the real world.

The "real world" of the first third of the '70s, it will be recalled, included the ever-escalating Vietnam war and the ever-degenerating language flowing out of Washington. It was the Nixon era, the one that ended with Watergate. Perhaps in some indirect way of which I was not fully conscious, the degeneracy of language (and not only language) that was so evident a feature of the last years and final collapse of the Nixon presidency sapped my enthusiasm for the battle for clarity in analyzing the workings of religious language.

I could sympathize with the moral passion of Wittgenstein in the face of a similar situation of linguistic degeneracy in the last days of Hapsburg Vienna. It was the driving power of his philosophical work. I found instead that I was becoming increasingly bored by philosophical analysis. I therefore gave in to the urging of colleagues and accepted something I had carefully avoided all my life: administrative work. I took on the chairmanship of the religion department at Temple University in 1974.

For the next few years, I was engaged mostly with parenting: working to develop the cooperative spirit and patterns so necessary for a department of 20 specialists if we were to listen to and learn from each other in such a way that we could train graduate students together rather than at cross-purposes. Other university administrative tasks were also added, in the form of chairing a review of graduate programs in all of the colleges of the university. Teaching was reduced to a minimum and done mostly with the left hand. I found myself working almost exclusively as an academic administrator, and perhaps I would be doing that now, were it not for the fact that one particular administrative task played a central role in bringing about a change of mind.

Wrong About Israel

The first and primary job confronting me as chairman of the department was to shepherd the troops into making two appointments in Judaism to replace Jewish colleagues who had left us for other institutions. The process took us two years, and I spent a good deal of that time talking with Jewish scholars, reading about Judaism, and reading the works of and finally interviewing candidates. In the meantime, I had to make short-term appointments to keep our offerings in Judaism available for students. The first of these was Rivka Horwitz, visiting in the area from Israel. Just to see how things were working out, I visited her graduate seminar, and there I was introduced to Franz Rosenzweig's doctrine of creation, which struck me as exceptionally exciting and clearly a step ahead of what is usually said on the matter in the Christian tradition.

Rosenzweig, importantly, but also all those other contacts with the world of Jews and Judaism, opened my eyes to something I had been looking at somewhat casually all along but had never really seen: Israel, the Jewish people, the people of God, was definitely alive. "The synagogue," "Jewish legalism," and all those old slogans of our theological tradition came tumbling down like the house of cards they were. In their place, actual Judaism, the living faith of this living people of God, came into view. I was fascinated.

I was more than fascinated. In the midst of administrative chores taking more and more of my time, I was set to thinking furiously. The Christianity I knew said that what I was coming to see so clearly simply did not exist, had not existed since Jesus Christ. What I was discovering was something of which I had heard nothing as an undergraduate, seminarian or graduate student. Yes, I knew that Barth had said some highly original and interesting things about ancient Israel and even about the continuing Jewish entity, but the latter was not real. It was but a ghost of ancient Israel, kept alive in the world as only a shadow of something else.

What I was coming face to face with, however, was no shadow, no "indirect witness to Jesus Christ," but a fully historical (certainly "warts and all") living tradition, constituting a quite direct witness to the God of Israel. If Christian theology said that this did not exist, then Christian theology, at least on *this* point, was simply wrong. It was wrong about Israel, the people of God, and therefore it was to that extent wrong about the God of Israel, wrong about the God and Father of Jesus Christ. I was far more than fascinated; I was back at my old discipline, wrestling with fundamental issues of systematic theology. What would Christian theology look like if it were corrected at so central a point? Would it even be recognizable as Christian theology?

Willing to Speak the Language

I thus found myself drawn deeply into the two linguistic communities of the church and the Jewish people. Whatever my earlier difficulties in understanding the use of the word "God," I found that if I were to get anywhere with the problems now confronting me, I had to accept myself as a member of one of those two linguistic communities and therefore to speak with them of the God of whom they both spoke. My older problems did not receive any direct answers. They simply receded into the background; or rather, the position from which I had been asking them was no longer one on which I could stand if I were to take seriously this new (or very old) problem.

Instead, seen from within this tension between the church and the Jewish people, what before had been the problem of "God" now was the problem of *God* as the God of both of these realities. By entering into their common problem and conflict, I found myself able and willing to speak their language. All the old problems remained, but they now appeared to be philosophical problems, not half so burning as the theological ones. I had run into a paradox and an incoherence that made the philosophical ones seem positively trivial.

The task confronting me—indeed, confronting the whole of theology and the whole of the church, if it were ever to notice it—was therefore to understand and interpret what God had done in Jesus Christ that had resulted in the concurrent existence and history of the church and the Jewish people. Both were there, side by side. I had to understand how this had come about.

No church history I had ever been taught had so much as hinted at the real historical situation. And what was that Judaism of the post-Exilic period, which had produced not only Jesus of Nazareth, but also Yohanan ben Zakkai, and which was to flower in not just patristic Christianity but also, during precisely the same centuries, in Rabbinic Judaism? Clearly I had much to learn. I therefore escaped at the first decent moment, at the close of my first term as chairman, and went off to read for a year—and think.

The last third of the decade of the '70s was spent digesting, digging deeper and formulating for publication the results of the change of mind that took place during the middle third. The prolegomena, or things to be said first, of the larger (and multivolume) systematic reflection on the matter, subtitled "a theology of the Jewish-Christian reality," has already appeared (*Discerning the Way* [Seabury, 1980]). Rather than speculate about what lies ahead, however, I would rather focus now on my perceptions of my context and my work, as these have been influenced by my change of mind.

The Context for Doing Theology

Let me begin with the interesting contextual situation. Here I am at present, and as a result of the change, a self-confessed Christian systematic theologian working in a large department of religion in a state university. Does that make sense? Is that any place in which to do a theology that openly addresses itself to the church? Is that appropriate to a religion department, in contrast to a school of theology or a divinity school? And is this proper, constitutionally, in a state-supported university?

I have not had to appeal to that oldest and best argument for the institution of academic tenure, the unqualified freedom of a scholar to move as his or her research and thinking lead, without being bound by past assumptions or present colleagues. As we have developed our department, we have intentionally left open the possibility that teaching about religion might be carried on by those committed to a religious tradition. Indeed, at least some colleagues outside of our department seem not at all opposed to the discussion and articulation of real theology—in their terms, real religion—within what is, after all, a department of religion.

My response to the question, therefore, will be more substantive. If Christian theology, which may or may not be listened to by the church, needs to be done in full awareness of Jewish theology, as I now believe, and then in due course in awareness of Islamic theology, and eventually surely also in awareness of Indian, Chinese and Japanese traditions, then where better can it be done than in a context in which it must be hammered out in constant discussion with Jewish (and then Islamic, and then Eastern) colleagues and especially graduate students, whose interests—and in some cases commmitments—lie in these other traditions?

The history-of-religions point of view has no monopolistic right to be the only ground for the study of religion. If one is moved on *theological* grounds to take other traditions seriously, one has another and most fruitful approach to the study of one's own tradition in the presence of and in relation to other traditions. And where else but in such a department can a Christian theologian have the glorious if frightening responsibility of training, e.g., future Jewish theologians, as well as those who may contribute to turning the church toward new responsibilities?

As I see the matter, there is not in fact any constitutional issue at stake. When I conduct a seminar on, for example, Karl Barth's doctrine of revelation, none of my Jewish students need fear that I am trying to convert them to Christianity. Far from it. We are, rather, asking together how well Barth really understood *Torah* as good news to Israel (quite well, thank you), and how well he understood the teaching of the rabbis that Torah-living by the Jewish people was living by grace (quite poorly, I'm afraid), and whether the correction of his mistake could produce a better theology for Christian self-understanding and perhaps even something helpful for Jewish theology. *Mutatis mutandis*, in seminars on Franz Rosenzweig or Hermann Cohen, we are asking together about the adequacy and helpfulness of their work as theology for the Jewish people, and also what Christian theology has perhaps to learn from them. Does this in any way touch the constitutional prohibition of the establishment of religion?

My students are mostly Jewish and Christian, since the relationship between these two traditions is the center of my work, but we have given much thought to the relation of our traditions to the others, especially to Islam, which stands in a special relationship to ours for both historical and theological reasons. I think I might win some agreement from my students if I expressed a tentative understanding of the matter as follows. It may be that the God of Israel, as King of the Universe, is working his purposes out also in these other traditions—and in our situation, their reality confronts us regularly in the persons of faculty colleagues and graduate students.

We as Jews and Christians need in any case to work out our own self-understandings and understandings of God together, because we share the same name of God and largely the same canon of Scriptures, not to speak of subsequent history (although Jewish history in the world of Islam must be learned and not forgotten by Christians). We should do this, however, in such a way as to be open to the question of whether we can hear in these other traditions the voice we have been disciplined to hear by our own Scriptures. This is (with Schleiermacher *and* Barth) to deny the validity of the concept of natural or general religion, but (*with* Barth and *against* Schleiermacher) to learn to listen to our own Scriptures, in order (with *neither* Schleiermacher *nor* Barth) to listen to the Scriptures of other traditions with sensitive ears for the voice of the God we trust we know, perhaps even to hear a word that may correct our reading of our own Scriptures.

That, I am prepared to argue, is a fittingly scholarly investigation of religion in a department of religion in a state-supported university. May it go on elsewhere as well, but if not elsewhere, surely it can and should go forward where it is now taking place.

A Christian, Not a Jew

To return to the theme of this series, let me conclude with three points, the clarification of which will help define how my mind has changed in the past decade. The points are that I am now a Christian, doing systematic theology, not "Holocaust theology." First, I am a Christian, not a Jew. The more I learn about Judaism and the Jewish people, the clearer it becomes that I am not a Jew, not an "honorary Jew," not a Jew by adoption or election. I am a Gentile, a Gentile who seeks to serve the God of Israel because as a Christian I share in the call of that God to serve him in his church, alongside, not as part of, his people Israel. As a Gentile, I am bound to that God not by *Torah* but by Jesus Christ. That, as I see it, is not my decision but his, or it is mine only as an obedient acknowledgment of his.

Second, I have returned to the work I left off in the beginning of the '60s, the self-critical task of the church called systematic theology. I have now found a new lens, Judaism, through which to carry on this work, but I am finding Karl Barth once more to be a superbly stimulating and helpful teacher, especially at the points at which I must disagree with him. He is proving to be a better guide than Calvin, Luther, Thomas, Augustine, Athanasius and Irenaeus (with all of whom he was in continuous dialogue) because he was both more thorough and more rigorously systematic down to the smallest detail. He sets a standard for theological work for which we can only be grateful. When I disagree with him, he forces me to think hard and carefully. What more can one have from a teacher?

Finally, in the light of all that went on in the '70s, I must say that I do not in any way conceive of myself as a Holocaust theologian or a theologian of the Holocaust. The horror of the Holocaust has surely opened the eyes of many Christians to the reality of the Jewish people. I have told the story of how my eyes were opened, which was not by way of the Holocaust. What Christians need to see, in my judgment, is not the Holocaust, but that which lives after and in spite of the Holocaust, the living reality, "warts and all," of the Israel of God, the Jewish people.

What concerns me as a Christian theologian is whether Christians will come to see that the God and Father of our Lord Jesus Christ is still loved, revered and obeyed by his original love, the people of God, the Jews. And if most of them do not love and serve God, what shall we say about most of those who have been baptized? The reality of the Jewish people, fixed in history by the reality of their election, in their faithfulness in spite of their unfaithfulness, is as solid and sure as that of the Gentile church. That is what I ran into and had to see, and that is what accounts, as far as I can tell, for how my mind has changed in the past decade, and my agenda for the future.

JOHN B. COBB, JR.

A Critical View of Inherited Theology

The '60s were a shattering time for many of us. We were taught by blacks, Indians and Chicanos to read American history in a new way. The war in Vietnam forced us to look from unaccustomed perspectives at the role played by the United States in international affairs. On the one hand, this was for me a painful experience, forcing me to recognize the extent to which my identity was that of a white American, and making me aware of the extreme ambiguity of that identity.

On the other hand, the decade was not so difficult for me theologically. Whereas the radical theologies and the death-of-God theologies were threatening to many, it was all too easy for me to see these movements as attacking forms of Christian belief from which I had been weaned in my graduate school days at Chicago. Of course, I knew that my own form of faith was also being challenged, but the main impact I felt was a heightened responsibility to make clear that Christian faith in God did not depend on those ideas which were being most vigorously and justifiably attacked. My understanding of Christian faith was maturing, but I was not inwardly pressed in new directions. Indeed, my style of theology, which had been viewed with suspicion and contempt by the reigning neo-orthodoxy at the beginning of the '60s, was taken more seriously at the end.

Something Happened

It was not until the summer of 1969 that my complacency was shattered and I went through a conversion experience. As with many such conversions, the changes appeared more drastic at the time than they do in retrospect. Nevertheless, something did happen to me, and my work in the '70s was different because of it.

Up until then, despite my painful awareness of the many injustices in global society and the responsibility of the United States for some of them, I had assumed that the global movement which had eventuated in independence for so many countries was leading to their economic development also. The task, I thought, was to encourage greater generosity on the part of developed nations so as to speed up the process of development elsewhere. My son, Cliff, who was then 18 years old, had earlier come to a deep awareness of the global problem and had prodded me from time to time to think again. But until the summer of 1969 I had assimilated the new data he provided into the old world view.

That summer, quite abruptly, I was forced to the awareness that the structures of society and the patterns of development which I had taken largely for granted are leading humanity toward global self-destruction. Until then I had supposed that, despite all the evils in the world—oppression, war, torture, starvation—humanity had time to work toward their solution. That summer I realized that the very ways in which "progress" was being made—e.g., dominant development policies as well as economic programs in the industrialized world—were all part of the total network of processes that were destroying the basis of human life on the planet. The issue of human survival seemed so overwhelming in its importance that I felt I must reorient my priorities at once.

My first practical response was to work with others at the School of Theology at Claremont to organize a conference in April 1970 to relate theology to this issue. Our topic was "A Theology of Survival." My little book *Is It Too Late? A Theology of Ecology* grew out of a paper I wrote for that conference as well as other speeches I was making in those days. But it was clearly not enough to call attention to the problem and to point out the needed theological changes. Proposals for action were required also, but the search for appropriate proposals led to discouragement.

While the majority of writers continued to suppose that no real changes were needed, the minority who shared my view that the world was heading for disaster had little to offer in terms of constructive suggestions. We were dismissed by most as prophets of doom, and too often those few who heard what we were saying fell into despair. Neither complacency nor despair could contribute to the needed repentance.

It seemed then, and it seems now, that we must have images of a hopeful future. Some of us hunted earnestly for someone who might have something positive to say. We were shocked to find so little. We found that a tiny handful of lonely economists were discussing alternatives to a growth society. A California group was making thoughtful plans for what the state could be like in the year 2000. And a visionary architect in Arizona was projecting architectural ecologies (or "arcologies") which could use the earth's resources more frugally while providing a more humane context for urban life. We held a second conference in May 1972 on "Alternatives to Catastrophe" at which the economist Herman Daly and the architect Paolo Soleri shared their hopeful visions with us.

A Basic Continuity

Nothing has happened in the years since 1969 to change my mind with respect to the importance of the new realization that dawned upon me then. A manuscript on explanation and causation in history, which my conversion led me to lay aside 90 per cent completed, still sits on a shelf. I have continued to speak and write and participate in conferences where it has been possible to share my concerns. The School of Theology at Claremont has tried to integrate a sense of the global crisis into its curriculum and its community life. For several years I had the rare opportunity to work with Jitsuo Morikawa, who led the American Baptists into a nationwide program on "Evangelistic Life Styles" which took seriously and realistically our global context and crisis. In the summer of 1979 at MIT I participated in the World Council of Churches' Conference on Faith, Science and the Future, which was committed to envisioning a just, participatory and sustainable society.

As I look back now, it is clear that my conversion, though real, falls within a more basic continuity. For one thing, conversion to global survival concerns did not uproot me from my Christian faith. It did make me view the historical forms of faith more critically, for I could not doubt that Christian doctrine had contributed to the insensitivity to the nonhuman world that now threatens to destroy the human world as well. But as I explored the archaic and Eastern doctrines to which others in the environmental movement sometimes turned, I found them inadequate. To me it seemed, and seems, that Christianity has much to learn from others, but that an enriched and transformed Christianity can best guide us through our crisis.

In the second place, I discovered that the philosophy of Alfred North Whitehead, which since graduate school days had been so important in shaping my formulations of Christian faith, already contained the sensi-tivities called for in the new situation. Indeed, passages in Whitehead and in the writings of my teacher, Charles Hartshorne, which I had pre-viously passed over without comprehending, now leaped out at me. In-stead of needing to look elsewhere for a way of articulating my thought after my conversion, I felt a fresh excitement in returning to the same sources. I became more of a Whiteheadian than before.

Thinking Holistically

In the third place, although my immediate response to the conversion was to focus on the global issue in a way that shunted many theological and philosophical questions to one side, I came rapidly to realize that it is precisely the separation of issues and topics from one another that is the deepest cause of our global sickness. We must think holistically, break-ing down the barriers between the disciplines. The most abstract thought is often the most concretely relevant when it is truly understood and ap-propriated, and efforts to be immediately relevant often do more harm than good.

Hence most of the projects that commanded my attention before the conversion have seemed to me appropriate to take up again in the past decade. I am convinced that the tasks now confronting the Christian thinker are vast. I am troubled that so much of the energy of professional Christian theologians seems currently to be invested in technical, histori-cal and methodological questions. These are important, but when they become absorbing, this importance becomes invisible.

I am glad that blacks and women and Latin Americans have, through-out the decade, been demanding that theology be so formulated as to call for and advance human liberation. I cannot identify with any one form of liberation theology, and insofar as they are separated from the technical, historical and methodological questions dealt with by the "establish-ment," these theologies suffer incompleteness. But I can hardly doubt that it is in these forms that theology today has authenticity and vitality. We cannot move toward global salvation without hopeful images of the future, and no image is hopeful which does not picture all groups as able to shape their own destinies. If we cannot think past the conflicting goals of different groups to the world in which their diverse interests can be reconciled, too much energy will be spent on bickering among those who should be allies in a common struggle. It is not yet clear whether we are able to grasp or be grasped by the hopeful images we need.

Even this is not enough. The thinking that could guide us out of our morass must be integrative thinking, not only about social goals but also in relation to the whole range of the sciences. Many of the sciences need new models both for their separate work and for their relation to one another. They continue, in too many cases, to dehumanize the sensibilities and imaginations of those who study them. This effect is associated with the too-great readiness of scientific practitioners to sell their skills and their discoveries for uses that reinforce patterns of global oppression. A better model for quantum physics or the sought-for unification of quantum and relativity theory would not be merely an interesting theoretical development but a stage in the reshaping of the human mind that could help to free us from the enervating fragmentation that now blocks creative responses. In short, Christians should not be indifferent to the imaginative vision of such theoretical physicists as David Bohm.

Finding the Way

In addition to the relation of Christian thought to the sciences, we must turn our attention to the relation of Christian thought to the other great religious Ways of humankind. We live in a world in which we Christians can consider our Way only one Way among others, and yet we cannot give up the claim to a certain ultimacy and universality with respect to that Way which is Jesus Christ. This is for me a central theological problem, and my book *Christ in a Pluralistic Age* was an attempt to deal with it.

Whereas during the '60s I thought in terms of an ultimate choice between different Ways, in the '70s I have been trying to think past such a decision. I want to see how the parochial Christian Way we have inherited can be transformed, in faithfulness to Christ, into a Way which includes the truth of other Ways, and can therefore come to be what it now is not—*the* Way.

My work on this problem has been chiefly in relation to Mahayana Buddhism, and my encounter with the great thinkers of that tradition has been, next to the global crisis to which I have referred, the greatest source of change in my thought. The truth of Buddhism provided me with a second perspective from which to view our inherited theology critically, but thus far it has confirmed me in my faith in Christ and also in my conviction of the continuing fruitfulness of Whitehead's philosophy for responding to crucial issues of our time.

No one in seminary education can have been unaffected in the '70s by the surge of women into ministry and by the theological issues that women are raising. The feminist challenge to inherited Christian teaching may be more fundamental than that of the global crisis or other religious Ways. I have not given this challenge the sustained attention I have devoted to the other two, partly because the task is being ably carried on by women theologians. But I cannot speak of how my mind has changed in the '70s without testifying to the repeated jolts I have received from this quarter. Step by step I have been forced to realize how very patriarchal indeed our tradition has been, at levels far deeper than language, and to how great an extext my own thinking had been unconsciously shaped by masculine biases. Still, I have concluded here too that a transformed Christianity is more able to guide us than a new feminist religion, and that Whitehead's philosophy is a fruitful aid in overcoming the masculine bias of our heritage.

My conviction of the continued fruitfulness of Whitehead's philosophy has deepened along with my awareness that the tasks confronting Christian thought are far beyond the capacities of any one person. To encourage wide participation, David Griffin and I established the Center for Process Studies. Since 1973, the center has been a major part of my life. Its function is to stimulate interreligious, intercultural and interdisciplinary reflection, aiming toward more inclusive modes of thought. It has sponsored conferences with Buddhists, Vedantists, Chinese philosophers, biologists, neurophysiologists, physicists, political philosophers and feminists, as well as with Christian ethicists, theologians and biblical scholars. Conferences are now planned on aesthetics, the Holocaust and education. There have been some encouraging spin-offs. The new patterns of thinking needed for our time cannot be stage-managed by anyone.

To place Christian thinking in the straitjacket of church theology is a serious mistake. Christians should think in the service of all creation and in relation to the deepest challenges to the gospel. Such thought could, of course, be understood as "church theology," but the tendency of that rubric is to focus attention upon the traditions and current life of the church in a way that is too limiting. Nevertheless, Christians must be concerned about the church and, quite specifically, about those particular denominations and congregations with which they are involved. I have been deeply concerned about the disease of the church at a time when it has such remarkable opportunities for global leadership. It seems today that in order to elicit vitality and sacrificial commitment,

American churches must preach idolatry. That is, they must call for wholehearted devotion to quite fragmentary truths and goals.

Some churches refuse to do this. They remain open to the wider range of truth and formulate more inclusive goals. But these churches are not able to present a sufficiently convincing vision of what faith is, or of purposes worth living for, to evoke more than fragmentary commitment. The tendency in these churches—the ones with which I am most closely associated—is to identify a number of worthwhile goals and to devise a variety of loosely related programs and strategies for moving toward them. But the skills these churches require and the conceptualities they use to understand what they are doing have only a vague relation to Christian faith.

We need total devotion to that which is worthy of total devotion—that is, to God as related to all things. As a church we lack the vision or the understanding to evoke that devotion. In large part the fault lies in the failure of us Christian theologians to deal adequately with the intellectual and cultural issues of our time. Hence my concern for the church leads me to redouble my efforts to encourage more unifying modes of thought and to wrestle with the meaning of Christian doctrine in that context.

But this concern has led me also to try occasionally to deal directly with the meaning of a holistic faith for the practical day-by-day life of Christian churches. I have spoken and written on spirituality and published a booklet on theology and pastoral care. But the task here too is vast, and I can personally contribute very little. I am pleased that those most directly dealing with the practice of professional ministry and the life of Christian churches are expressing a renewed sense of urgency to achieve Christian integrity at a level deeper than the verbal. I look to others for leadership but hope to contribute what I can.

An Ecological Model

I count myself fortunate that through much of this decade I have had a happy collaboration with the Australian biologist Charles Birch. Apart from him, the work of the Center for Process Studies with leading biologists and physicists would have been very difficult to initiate. He is chiefly responsible for the conference which resulted in the publication of *Mind in Nature*. Birch shares with me both the Christian faith and the influence of Whitehead's philosophy, as well as keen concern about the global disaster toward which the still-dominant trends are leading us.

We are now finishing a joint manuscript tentatively titled *The Liberation of Life: From Cell to Community.* We want to show that philosophy can help biologists to develop an ecological model of living things that will both be more fruitful scientifically and give more appropriate guidance to ethics and social policy. We believe that our book points to a way of thinking of God that can help enliven Christian faith as well. It is indeed a dangerous matter in these days of specialization to deal with so many fields, but for all its limitations the book embodies the effort to attain to a more holistic vision. I hope it will encourage others to carry on that effort.

JAMES M. GUSTAFSON

A Theocentric
Interpretation of Life

In my circumstances, the title "How My Thinking Has Been Developing" would be preferable for this series to "How My Mind Has Changed." The latter assumes that an author has "made up his mind" and is interested in checking carefully what he or she said in the past and, like St. Augustine, in making retractions. The notion of making retractions seems to require that at a later stage one has arrived at Truth, and that thus there is a clear standard for judging earlier errors. Perhaps the editors were not expecting that to occur. I shall not cite quotations from my previous work which are no longer accurate expressions of my present thinking; I have no interest in doing so.

This article has a pattern. The form is somewhat like the plan of the city of New Delhi. The British planned a good bit of the city around the huge Connaught Circle, into which arteries of traffic flow from all directions. In this article I initially take one artery after another to the outer rim of the circle. Then I go around the circle a few times, and in the end indicate how I, at least, take my bearings. The circle we might call theocentricity.

Some recollection is required even to respond to my revision of the series title. Certainly it is the case that I was very interested for a number of years in trying to develop methods for Christian ethics that would correct the simplistic Christian moralisms to which Protestantism has been addicted for a long time. There were at least two fronts being attended to in this enterprise: the importance of taking very seriously the kinds of precise and technical information required to make particular judgments and choices (while not losing sight of the difficulties in getting accurate information and ideologically unbiased interpretation), and the importance of making the moral arguments of Christians more rigorous both philosophically and theologically. I was attracted to Paul Ramsey's work because he clearly shared these purposes, though we have worked them out differently; I was interested in Roman Catholic moral theology and social ethics for similar reasons, though again the execution of a similar purpose is different.

I do not regret the attention I gave to those matters, and I admire many of my colleagues who have pursued similar purposes with rigor and diligence beyond my capacities to achieve. Many of them now call themselves "religious ethicists," and therein lies a clue to some dissatisfaction. Those who have taken the garb of "religious studies," and who have either left behind any serious personal religious interests or valiantly hold them in abeyance, are doing important analytical work on religious ethics—work that I continue to do in seminars. Some, however, have become practical moral philosophers, moral problem-solvers, and it is not clear to what the adjective "religious" refers. Against my friends and colleagues, and even against myself, I have fired this arrow previously in an article published in *Commonweal*, and I shall not use another arrow on the same target.

The issue, however, persists: What makes ethics religious? Several things can be said to do so: the fact that one is working from the lore of a particular religious tradition; the seriousness of the attention and intention with which one is concerned about morality; the openness to larger dimensions that affect morality, like world views, metaphysics or ontology. Or it might be that moral life is related to God, and ethics to theology.

Ethics and Anthropocentrism

For more than a decade the practical area that primarily occupied my attention was that of biological research and medicine. I believe it was in 1960 that I first delivered lectures on ethics to medical students at Yale. That interest was substantive and real, though its lasting benefits to me might well be the problems which most work in that area comes up to and then ignores. I have tried to encourage the casuists—whether physicians, scientists, philosophers, ex-theologians or continuing theologians—to take some of these problems into account.

For example, every particular question in critical cases of medical ethics involves some choices regarding what we value about human life. What is it we value? What is the normatively human? Why do we value what we value? Why do we say that persons have rights? What is the ground of these rights? If these questions do not drive one to theology, they at least drive one to the secular first cousins of theology. And if traditional ways of answering these questions—for instance, in classic natural-law theory—are not sufficient, how do we go about finding better answers? And why are they better?

Developments of Western culture have increasingly tended toward anthropocentrism. That history has been written by a number of scholars. One line of argument goes that it is biblical faith that has contributed to the demystification of nature, robbing it of the religious or spiritual significance it had not only in primitive animistic cultures, but also in ancient Greek and Roman cultures, and has yet in Asian cultures. This liberation of nature, a necessary effect of the Bible's transcendent God, enabled humanity to "thingify" it, to see its utility value, to take from it any inherent teleology, not to mention an ultimate purpose in relation to God other than its meeting of human needs.

Certain interpretations of the Bible, and certain interpretations of the hierarchy of beings in our culture, have reinforced the notion that the rest of the creation exists for the benefit of our species—a species that has evolved relatively recently in paleontological perspectives. The increase of human capacities to describe and explain the operations of nature and of human society has been turned to instrumental usage, and we have seen the ascendance of "technical reason." The time and space scopes of the consequences of human interventions into nature and into social processes have expanded without the commensurate increase in humility that is proper, given the continuing remarkable limitations of foreknowledge of long-range consequences and of the capacity to control them. The human being becomes both the measurer of all things and the measure of all things—at humankind's own peril, we need to add, and to the peril of the creation of which humankind is a minuscule part.

"All traditional ethics is anthropocentric," wrote that wise first cousin of theologians, Hans Jonas; at least traditional Western ethics has had a strong tendency toward anthropocentrism. Teleologies have been in focus on what is the good for humans, and not for the whole of the creation; frequently they have been in focus on what is the good for individuals, and not even the common good of the human community. The difficulty of knowing the latter itself becomes an excuse for not seeking to find it, and the historical evidences of injustices and tyrannies that have occurred when persons who thought they knew it gained power warn us properly against its perils. Modern secular ethics has had good episte-mological reasons for doubting whether we could know an objective moral order even if there is one, and has devised sophisticated tech-niques for formulating the principles of moral action without recourse to "metaphysics" or anything that looks remotely like it.

Yet it is events that move many of our contemporaries to what might well be intellectually primitive impulses toward recognition of the need to enlarge the range of considerations involved in ethics, to see individu-als in relation not only to other individuals but also to communities, to see our actions in relation not only to historical events, but also to the wider natural world. While I am not persuaded that we can know the moral order of nature with the certainty that some Roman Catholic phi-losophers and moral theologians have thought we could, I am persuaded that a turn in ethical thinking is required, if not from humanity to God, at least from humanity to the signs of an ordering of life which is objective to individuals, objective to communities of persons, and objective to our species.

A Theocentric Orientation

During this period I have found myself making a move that the gen-eration of my teachers made in the 1920s and 1930s. Religion had be-come terribly subjective; its object, God, seemed to be left out. My per-ceptions of a great deal of religious activity in the past two decades is that it is highly instrumental—not for the purpose of honoring God and of-fering gratitude to him, but for the purpose of inducing subjective states in humans. Even the great Christian theme of redemption has been re-duced to a psychological principle: you are accepted. By whom? On what basis?

And, as has been the case so often in Christian history, religion be-comes instrumental to moral ends chosen for other than religious rea-sons. When we give the examples of anticommunism and nationalism, all of us cheer and say Amen. But the same principle has been at work in movements for radical social change. The most vulgar form is the "pray-in"; the sophisticated forms are more profoundly theological: a moral end or a moral interest becomes the hermeneutical device for interpret-ing the Bible or theological themes that can be grounded in the Bible. If we can find a way to make religion or God serve our subjective ends, whether they be to help us feel better or to change the world, we use them.

Certainly religion in all times and all cultures has had utility value; in the biblically grounded religions of the West, however, the ultimate end has been theocentrically oriented, turned toward an objective reality. Moses and the prophets, Jesus and Paul, Augustine and Thomas Aquinas, the great 16th century Reformers, the Puritans, Jonathan Edwards and others—they were correct in the primary intuition that religion deals with the relations of humans and the world to God and to his purposes. Those rebels against religious subjectivism earlier in our century—Barth and Brunner, Wieman and H. Richard Niebuhr and others—had a similar primary intuition, and it was correct.

I have, since adolescence, been persuaded that cultural and historical relativism was more valid than the efforts to shed our various layers of skin so that we could achieve pure disinterestedness, rational autonomy in morality, and pure objectivity in other areas of knowledge. No doubt my growing up in an immigrant sectarian religious community contributed to that opinion, as did my service in Burma and India during World War II, studies of sociology and anthropology as an undergraduate, my reading of Troeltsch under the aegis of a great teacher, James Luther Adams, and other things. It was H. Richard Niebuhr's *The Meaning of Revelation* that made more theological sense to me than the process theology that dominated the Federated Theological Faculty of the University of Chicago in my years as a Bachelor of Divinity student.

I am somewhat amused that Roman Catholic theologians, a lot of Protestants, and sociologists of religion are only now learning about sociology of knowledge and its significance for theology, about "historical" mentalities and such things. Different persons and different groups are not, in that terrible current term, "in phase" because they are the bearers of the cultures and beliefs from which they come. But when persons begin to call any set of symbols—any beliefs which give meaning and coherence to life—a "theology," I wish they would instead talk about the functional equivalents to theology. (I suppose, though, that if philosophers are no longer lovers of wisdom, theologians no longer should be expected to be thinking about God.)

Surely all religions do function to provide meaning to experience; descriptively there is nothing wrong with that. But surely in the Western religious traditions those meanings relate all things to God, and when the properly descriptive becomes the basis for prescriptions for religious life, the reduction transforms Christianity and Judaism almost to the point of unrecognizability. Relativism without relation to an ultimate object degenerates into religious subjectivism; i.e., there are no bases for making judgments about the adequacy of religious views other than how satisfying they are to those who share them. When relative traditions do not test themselves by more generalizable criteria, they become defensive, smug and incorrigible.

Honest in Regard to Culture

The work of Stephen Toulmin and others has given me strong bases for believing what I always suspected as a relativist—namely, that the development of the sciences as historical movements is not unlike the development of theology, and that while the sciences have different and more satisfactory ways to adduce evidences that sustain their theories than does theology, the truth claims they make are not as "hard" as was sometimes thought to be the case. A theologian can respond to this work in two ways: one can say with satisfaction and glee that the sciences are in their own way relativistic and even "confessional" and so theology is liberated from its presumed archaism. But one can also say that theology, like the developments in particular sciences, has to be prepared to make its own revisions of those theories that have provided past ways of construing the world—ways that are no longer tenable.

The previous paragraph is not without its point with reference to the outcome of several of the paragraphs prior to it. Religion has an "objective reference," in piety called God. But the kind of retreat into biblical theology that some of the generation of my teachers made in order to recover the object of love and faith, the ultimate limiter and the condition of possibilities for life, is not a defensible retreat for me. At the same time it is the case that I am a religious thinker in the Christian tradition; I could not chuck that out if I tried. So the theological problem is the one that has been present since at least the Apologists (and really, in the Scriptures also); namely, how does a community working for good reasons within a historically particular tradition think about the object of its reverence, respect and gratitude in ways that can be honest with reference to its own culture and time?

Theological ethics has consistently been the area that I have most relished. I have taken generations of graduate students through classic texts and through important contemporary texts that have related God to morality, theology to ethics. We have together worked through these texts with systematic issues in view: Christian love; sin as a religious and moral term; love and justice; persons as moral agents; and the like. We have worked through Karl Barth and Thomas Aquinas side by side—to historians a scandalous way to teach—to sort out the fundamental options for relating theology to ethics. We have worked through important texts in a given period for comparative purposes, such as the Reformation (the Anabaptists get "equal time"); we have analyzed developments in Roman Catholic ethics in the modern period to see how and why they have changed; we have looked carefully at the works of a single author—for example, Jonathan Edwards. We have examined the ethics in the Bible, writings about the ethics in the Bible, and constructive biblical ethics with the same analytical agenda. We have studied various moral philosophers in conjunction with theologians. My route to theology has been and is the route of ethics. But that route always leads to theology.

Classic religious texts provide for me more joy and more use than most contemporary writings. It is more difficult, more fun and more profitable to think about my agenda for theology and ethics by reading the Bible, Augustine, Thomas Aquinas, Calvin, Luther, Edwards, Schleiermacher and Barth than it is to keep up with all the good books published by Orbis, Paulist, Westminster, Fortress, Abingdon, Eerdmans and Seabury presses. There are novel circumstances in the relations of theology and ethics, but no novel issues.

My attention has not been as parochial as the preceding paragraphs might suggest. For some years I worked with significant concentration on the Jewish legal and ethical tradition; in preparation for lectures delivered in various Indian universities I spent a year attempting to grasp some of the major features of religion, morality and history in that complex culture. To read again the classic tradition from Homer forward, and to be stimulated in my reflections about it by the work of Arthur W. H. Adkins and others, has been enormously beneficial. To have had the personal intellectual companionship of some colleagues from genetics, clinical medicine, psychiatry, philosophy, law, literature, social sciences and other fields has been a valuable gift that the University of Chicago and the professional communities of the city have provided. Similar contacts of comparable length and depth took place during the years of my more intimate participation in the work of the Hastings Center. My convictions about theology and ethics are being forged not only on the anvil of classics of the Christian tradition, but also by the hammers of pleasant and sometimes intensive cross-disciplinary contacts.

Items for an Agenda

I have rather cryptically referred to the agenda for theology and ethics. What are its items? I have worked it out most systematically in the last chapter of *Protestant and Roman Catholic Ethics: Prospects for Rapprochement* (University of Chicago Press, 1978). Briefly and in summary, it includes the following theses and items: Any systematic and comprehensive account of theological ethics has to have an organizing perspective, metaphor or principle. That "discrimen" (to use Robert Clyde Johnson's term for such) must relate coherently four base points: theology in the restricted sense of an understanding of God and his purposes in relation to the world; an interpretation of the meaning and significance of "the world"; an interpretation of persons as moral agents and of their acts; and an interpretation of how persons ought to make moral choices and moral judgments. In doing this, the author must make judgments about the adequacy of a proposed position with reference to four sources: the historically identifiable Christian tradition; philosophical methods, insights and principles; scientific information that is relevant and reasonably solid; and human experience broadly conceived.

Just as the "discrimen" makes a critical difference in how the base points are ordered, so does the preference for one of the base points as being most significant. Another critical choice is which of the four sources is most important and finally determinative when resolutions of issues between the four sources are made. Systematic and comprehensive theological ethics, I have argued, touches all the base points and uses all the sources in one way or another.

I am confident that this agenda and its items provide a very useful analytical framework for studying the theological ethics of a religious tradition. I am not nearly so confident that it is within my powers to develop a cogent, pursuasive, constructive account of theological ethics that meets the tests of adequacy and coherence that the agenda requires. Nonetheless, that is the task to which I have turned my attention.

A Natural Piety

This all sounds terribly cerebral and abstract, as if one were arranging information according to concepts, and interpreting them with some basic principle or metaphor. And so it would be if another deep conviction were not introduced—namely, that religion is basically a matter of the affections, in that rich 18th century sense of the term that Jonathan Edwards used; that it is a matter of piety (not piousness or pietism), in the rich sense that both St. Augustine and Calvin affirmed. Religion is an aspect or dimension of experience, and while that aspect can be described to a considerable extent, and some reasons be given to explain it, it is never susceptible to the kind of full, disinterested, rational justification that would be desirable for some apologetic purposes.

On this critical item for my current work I have already declared myself in *Can Ethics Be Christian?* (University of Chicago Press, 1975). That this assertion sounds "spooky" and esoteric to a number of my distinguished contemporaries, I know; that there is a natural piety in many persons similar to that about which Calvin was certain, I am willing to argue. (Indeed, I find four significant impulses to be present in many of my "secularized" friends: a natural piety in the sense of a gratitude and respect for the givenness of "the world," a recognition that there are some dimly perceived orderings of life to which human activity must in some sense be conformed, an awareness of a human defect, and a muted honoring of Another about which not much is said.)

It is not only the acknowledgment of the priority of piety or affections in religion that leads me back to such classic theologians as Augustine, Calvin, Edwards and Schleiermacher; it is also their intimations and declarations of a very sovereign power who sustains and limits us as humans. It is their powerful portrayals of a shared theme—namely, that the destiny of the world is not in human hands—that make them theologically important to me, though with some critical themes that they generally share I have deep disagreements. And with the first three named I share a deep sense of the miseries and defects of human life. (A psychiatrist friend attributes much of this to a north Scandinavian view of the world, and wonders how Christian it really is.)

What in very general terms these theologians share which I find persuasive for many reasons is the primacy of piety, evoked by the powers of the Deity, and a sense that there are no clear resolutions of human ambiguities and, in the strongest technical sense, human tragedies in our temporal lives. They all sense that the conduct of human affairs requires conformity to an ordering of both possibilities and constraints ultimately grounded in the purposes of God. While Christian faith and life had for all of them their benefits, and while they did not hesitate to seek to persuade persons to take the Christian faith seriously because it guaranteed what they thought was in the best self-interests of humans (thus instrumentalizing Christianity), each in his own way proclaimed that the chief end of humanity, and indeed of the whole of the creation, was to honor, celebrate, glorify God.

How God Is Properly Honored

There is a lot of celebration going on in Christian circles. I suppose it is those who have most deeply felt the inhibitions of moralistic Christianity, in Protestant or Catholic forms, who insist on religion's making one feel good, and who want Christians to enjoy life. There is a lot of "piety" around that is also unrelated to morality in any effective and serious way. What a selective retrieval of theological tradition can express and enable us to see is that gratitude and honor to God, the forms of piety, require that we relate to all things appropriate to their relations to God—a phrase I have taken and slightly revised from the writings of my close friend Julian N. Hartt. The honoring of God is not the emotive impulse for taking morality seriously; God is properly honored only as humans seek in their actions and their relations to relate to all things appropriate to their relations to God.

Piety in my theological "construing of the world" (another turn of phrase which I owe to Hartt) does not take one beyond morality; the Deity whose majesty evokes piety is the ultimate power that sustains and orders the universe. And there is no guarantee that facing the limits of my finitude, ordering life according to some principles which are grounded in God's governance, will make me feel good, meet my short-range or even long-range interests, keep suffering from my doorstep or anyone's, or adequately explain it away, or bring compensatory justice to bear in some world to come. Piety—gratitude, honor, reverence and respect to God—demands from its most interior wellsprings the disciplining of life, the ordering of human communities, the relating of human activity and culture to the natural world in ways that recognize both human finitude and the human defect, and recognizes that life must be conformed to that ordering activity of God which we cannot fully know.

To state these interests, and to work out a coherent position that reflects them, requires selectivity with reference to the materials from the Christian tradition. But then, what theologian has not been selective? It requires selection of themes even from those theologians who most deeply inform one's thought and experience. E. R. Dodds, in *The Greeks and the Irrational* (University of California Press, 1951), cites an apt passage from an article by W. H. Auden:

> If we talk of tradition today we no longer mean what the eighteenth century meant, a way of working handed down from one generation to the next; we mean a consciousness of the whole of the past in the present. Originality no longer means a slight modification of one's

immediate predecessors; it means the capacity to find in any other work of any date or locality clues for the treatment of one's own subject matter [pp. 237–238].

Adequacy to Human Experience

If one emended the presumption that any of us can have a consciousness of the whole of the past, and the intimation that originality seems to be desirable, this statement expresses well my own response to the traditions to which I have sought to expose myself. It is one's own subject matter, and the attempt to deal with it responsibly in one's own time and place, that determines one's selection and use of materials from the Christian and other traditions. When the chips are down, it is adequacy to human experience—not just individual, but that of those whose experience is similar to one's own—that is decisive. That experience is deeply informed by traditions, by contemporary events in culture and society, by scientific and other intellectual enterprises of the modern world; one is not talking about minimal sensations. The best one can expect to do is speak honestly for oneself, with some confidence that one's own experience is not utterly unique but similar to that of a significant number of persons.

During my three years as a graduate student at Yale I was pastor of a small Congregational church; it was a rich and formative experience. When one sat up most of a night with a family that was bearing the grief of a suicide, or when one was responsible to preach to a group of people in the village, all of whom one knew very well, theological studies had to be forged into an honest way of interpreting not only the experiences of human suffering, but the threats of McCarthyism and the cold war, and the proposals to rezone a rural village in the face of the coming suburbanization. Such coherence as my theological and ethical thinking had then, has ever had, and has now, has come in significant measure from trying to make sense of human life in the light of that measure of the knowledge of God that can be affirmed. Although I seldom preach or conduct public worship, it continues to be the case that my most generalized thought comes in relation to a broad range of quite specific human experiences. And so at this stage, toward the end of my career, I continue to work at expressing and defending a theocentric interpretation of life, and particularly of moral activity. To this task I am by now fated.

WOLFHART PANNENBERG

God's Presence in History

Anyone engaged in the systematic construction of ideas should react with puzzlement to an invitation to report on the change of his or her mind. As with any other human being, it is only natural that such change occurs. But in the constructive thought of a systematic thinker, admission of change seems to indicate an acknowledgment of inadequacy and error. Therefore, it often occurs that such persons overestimate the degree of continuity in their own thought—and the reader may find me guilty of a similar fault.

On the other hand, even systematic human thought develops in time and can never be complete. An awareness of this fact and of the limitations it entails is itself a condition of the credibility of any system of ideas, and that may finally be so because time belongs to the essence of truth and of reality itself.

Nevertheless, when I search my memories and other evidence, I find it difficult to discern any fundamental change in my theological perspective since 1959, when I published an article on "Redemptive Event and History." It was the first public evidence of the project that had gradually taken shape in my mind during the preceding years: to work out on the level of systematic theology that ancient Israelitic view of reality as a history of God's interaction with his creation, as I had internalized it from the exegesis of my teacher Gerhard von Rad, after I had discovered how to extend it to the New Testament by way of Jewish eschatology and its developments by Jesus' message and history. When I began to understand that one should not set history and eschatology, nor (therefore) history and God, in opposition to one another, the general direction of my further thought was determined.

And yet, it never occurred to me simply to draw conclusions from such a premise. Rather, I found myself attracted to the searching study of the actual world of human experience and of the Christian tradition in the confident expectation of retrieving there the evidence of God's action that I assumed to be constitutive of all finite reality. Thus there were many occasions for changes of opinion in later years, but these changes were not in the least comparable to those that had occurred before.

To Probe the Christian Tradition

The most incisive change of mind happened when I became a Christian. Since I had not enjoyed the privilege of being raised in a Christian family, commitment to the study of Christian theology could not come about by a smooth and imperceptible process. Nor did it follow from a unique experience of conversion. Rather, it was the result of a series of experiences.

The single most important experience occurred in early January 1945, when I was 16 years old. On a lonely two-hour walk home from my piano lesson, seeing an otherwise ordinary sunset, I was suddenly flooded by light and absorbed in a sea of light which, although it did not extinguish the humble awareness of my finite existence, overflowed the barriers that normally separate us from the surrounding world. Several months earlier I had narrowly escaped an American bombardment at Berlin; a few weeks later my family would have to leave our East German home because of the Russian offensive. I did not know at the time that January 6 was the day of Epiphany, nor did I realize that in that moment Jesus Christ had claimed my life as a witness to the transfiguration of this world in the illuminating power and judgment of his glory. But there began a period of craving to understand the meaning of life, and since philosophy did not seem to offer the ultimate answers to such a quest, I finally decided to probe the Christian tradition more seriously than I had considered worthwhile before.

When I began to study theology as well as philosophy at Berlin in 1947, I was not yet certain that I wanted to become a theologian rather than a philosopher. But I was impressed by the Barthians' emphasis on the sovereignty of God in his revelation, and it seemed self-evident to me that God was to be conceived of as utterly sublime and majestic if there was any God at all. When I came to Basel in 1950 to study under Karl Barth himself, I was almost convinced of the appropriateness of his approach.

On the other hand, I was troubled by the dualism involved in his revelational positivism. It seemed to me that the truly sovereign God could not be regarded as absent or superfluous in ordinary human experience and philosophical reflection, but that every single reality should prove incomprehensible (at least in its depth) without recourse to God, if he actually was the Creator of the world as Barth thought him to be. Increasingly it seemed to me inconsistent with that assumption that Barth presented God's revelation as if God had entered a foreign country instead of "his home," as the Gospel of John tells us (1:11). Therefore, I felt that my philosophy and theology should not be permitted to separate, but that within their unity it should be possible to affirm the awe-inspiring otherness of God even more uncompromisingly than Barth had done, since he returned to reasoning by analogy.

Turning Point

After I transferred to Heidelberg to complete my studies, my inclination to combine philosophy and theology was greatly encouraged by closer acquaintance with patristic thought. At the same time I came to realize that history presents that aspect of the world of our experience which, according to Jewish and Christian faith, reveals God's presence in his creation. In this discovery, I owed much to Karl Löwith's lectures on the theological rootage of modern philosophies of history as well as to Gerhard von Rad's interpretation of the Old Testament.

It was a decisive turning point. Until that late period in my theological studies I had been unable to make much sense of biblical exegesis. The subject matter that fascinated me was the reality of God and the consequences to be derived from the affirmation of that reality in philosophy and in dogmatics. But now historical experience, tradition and critical exegesis, together with philosophical and theological reflection on their content and implications, became the privileged medium to discuss the reality of God. That meant that there is no direct conceptual approach to God, nor from God to human reality, by analogical reasoning, but God's presence is hidden in the particulars of history. In the regular meetings of a circle of friends at Heidelberg, after almost ten years of discussions, we finally arrived at the conclusion that even God's revelation takes place in history and that precisely the biblical writings suggest this solution of the key problem of fundamental theology.

Before that conclusion could be reached, a new way of relating the person and history of Jesus to the Old Testament's theology of history was required. That approach was found in apocalyptic thought, then commonly despised; further in a reassessment of the terminology related to "revelation" and of its history; and finally in an integration of all that with the problems of the philosophy of history. A new systematic category had to be explored (prolepsis) in order to describe the place of Jesus' history and especially of his resurrection within this framework, and in the end it became discernible that it is in history itself that divine revelation takes place, and not in some strange Word arriving from some alien place and cutting across the fabric of history.

This result, of course, could not fail to arouse violent and malign reactions from the leading schools of the day, Bultmannians as well as Barthians. It was as if we had committed a sacrilege. We were naïve enough then not to have expected any such reaction, but rather some enthusiastic acclamation.

Other Fields of Learning

Since that time, change and development have occurred on a different scale. The obligation of covering the entire field of systematic theology in my academic lectures brought to my attention not only new facts and perspectives, but also complete fields of learning that I had scarcely noticed before. They helped to put my theological project in a broader and more differentiated context. Thus I started to work out its implications for anthropology in an attempt to integrate the different disciplines of secular anthropology into a Christian interpretation of human nature and destiny that, in the context of contemporary thought, seemed to present the inevitable starting point for any attempt at theological reconstruction.

This concern alarmed some of my friends, as it seemed to indicate a shift in my general outlook, and in some way there was indeed a new picture emerging. But it was more a matter of methodological considerations in developing a systematic theology, together with explicit discussion of the implications involved in a program of "revelation as history." These implications being philosophical as well as theological in character, I spent considerable time and energy in exploring what the new concept of revelation meant to the problems of truth and knowledge in general as well as to the problems of a general theory of being and reality that, among other things, had to take account of the importance of the natural sciences in any serious concept of reality.

When I finally postponed the project of a comprehensive theological interpretation of human reason in order to confine myself to a particular section of it—the philosophy of science with special attention to the place of theology—there were again comments to the effect that a complete shift in my theological position had occurred. Many friends asked whether I could still identify with the position of my book *Jesus—God and Man*, the most obvious development and exposition of the program of *Revelation as History*. In my own mind, there was no question. I simply felt the obligation of working my way through those other regions in order to substantiate my claims concerning history, and especially that of Jesus as God's revelation.

Ecumenism and Universalism

Nevertheless, there were also real changes in the design itself. In the first place, I should mention the ecumenical experience. Since my early days as assistant at my teacher Edmund Schlink's Ecumenical Institute at Heidelberg and afterward during many years of regular ecumenical discussions, especially with Roman Catholic theologians, I became increasingly aware that Christian theology today should not limit itself to some narrowly defined confessional loyalty inherited from the past but should help to build the foundations of a reunited, if to some degree pluralistic, Christian church that should become more and more visible within the foreseeable future. This vision seems to match other universalistic aspects of the Christian tradition, especially its claim to universal reason, and it constitutes the most important practical application of my theological project.

Second, strong claims in some of my earlier statements concerning the universal intelligibility of God's revelation in Jesus Christ have been replaced by more restrained formulas that take more account of the intricacies of human language and belief. Of my original assertions, none encountered more uncompromising rejection than did my claims concerning the rationality of the Christian faith in God's revelation. Therefore, I felt obliged to ponder these criticisms with particular care, even if their polemical form made that more difficult than necessary.

What was the element of truth in such criticism? The result of my reflections was not a surrender of my claim to the rationality of faith but a revision of its form. If some of my early assertions sounded a bit triumphalistic, it may have been because of a too naïve way of referring to Scripture as fulfilled in Jesus Christ. As I revised my use of the idea of fulfillment of the Old Testament promises in Jesus Christ, I also developed more scrupulous ways of accounting for the truth-claims of the Christian tradition, including a more critical attitude toward the faith's tendency to dogmatism. This task also induced me to be more careful in my description of the relation between Christianity and Judaism.

To the degree that there was a change in my attitude, however, it meant an increase in critical rationality, rather than its limitation in order to make room for faith. I could never understand the argument that faith was in danger if it was in agreement with the judgment of true reason. I rather suspect that the real danger for faith lurks in its estrangement from rationality. But precisely the concern for rationality induced me to emphasize the provisional character of the knowledge of faith more than I did in earlier days.

Religious Language

Closely connected with this point is another: my sensitivity developed as to the functions of religious language that are not open to definitive proof or falsification, but nevertheless indicate in symbolic form the presence of the ultimate. Even in my early statements I emphasized that revelational history is always connected with language, and I tried to relate it to the ultimacy of the meaning claimed for a revelational event. Only on that assumption does it seem understandable why later interpretations can miss the meaning inherent in the events themselves. But my view on religious language was too narrow, and I too readily assumed that all religious language was transferred from secular use. Today I think that the religious dimension of human life is one of the irreducible roots of language, and I suspect that quite a few of our words developed from religious origins.

In recent years, the doctrine of God has taken more and more definitive shape in my thought. Whereas in earlier years God to me was the unknown God who came close only in Jesus Christ and could be approached only in him, "from below," but could not be adequately characterized in human language, I increasingly realized that there is other than conceptual language which nevertheless is not noncognitive.

Hence today I feel much more confident to develop a doctrine of God and to treat the subjects of Christian dogmatics in that perspective. That doctrine will be more thoroughly trinitarian than any example I know of. For many years I felt that the doctrine of God constituted the final task of Christian theology, although, of course, everything in it is related to God. Such a doctrine, however, seemed to presuppose a sufficient degree of clarity in many other areas, because talking about God involves everything else. Therefore, the appropriate way to present it will be in the form of a Christian systematic theology.

Religion Outlasts Ideology

I should not close without noting a change in my political attitudes. In my earlier years I had little doubt about not only the moral superiority but also the historical future of the values of the liberal democratic tradition. A little more than 15 years ago, I became considerably less optimistic. The course of the students' revolution in Europe, especially the unexpected susceptibility to Marxism on the part of many educated youth, made me more keenly aware of the unpredictability of irrational factors still shaping the course of history. In another way the political decline of the West in recent decades suggests similar conclusions.

However, the more insecure the future of a liberal, secular society appears to be, the more confident I feel about the future of religion—not a future in relation to emancipation and economic and/or political liberation. Much of the enthusiasm in such movements seems to me an unintentional contribution to accelerating the spread of oppressive regimes. But religion in the strict sense of the word can feel more secure today than it has for a long time. It will outlive every ideological regime. And the only serious challenge to Christianity will not be secular society, which is badly in need of religious support in our days, but rival religions.

SCHUBERT M. OGDEN

Faith and Freedom

The limits of self-analysis are obvious, and I shall not dwell on them. But as I look back over the past ten years of my life, I am impressed less by how my mind has changed than by how it has remained the same. True, I have already entered my sixth decade, and having thus become older, I should like to believe that I may also have become wiser. But if I have, it is by continuing to live and think along familiar lines, not by gradually or suddenly departing along strange ones. The proof of this, it seems to me, is that I have little trouble now in identifying with a statement I wrote for this journal in 1965, for an earlier series titled "How I Am Making Up My Mind." I find that most of what had, even then, proved constant in my thinking remains so, and that the working hypothesis I there committed myself to test continues to guide my reflections.

Issues of Action and Justice

Even so, my mind has changed in certain respects, as I have tried to indicate by the title I have given to this article. Like the title of the earlier piece, "Faith and Truth," it reflects my continuing conviction that there are and must be two poles to theological reflection insofar as the claims of Christian faith finally appeal for their credibility to our common experience as human beings. But whereas the word "truth" in the earlier title focused attention on the more theoretical aspect of such credibility, "freedom" in the present title is intended to point to the underlying human concern in which the concern for truth itself has its basis. In this way, I would like to signal what I myself sense to be a significant shift in my recent thinking: from being preoccupied for the most part with theoretical questions of belief and truth to giving greater attention to the practical issues of action and justice that likewise have their basis in the underlying concern for freedom.

This shift is occasioned largely by the challenge of the various theologies of liberation, whose influence I have increasingly felt since the early '70s as I have become convinced that it is by these theologies, as much as by any, that the cause of Christian theology is today being advanced. In this connection, I have been particularly struck by Gustavo Gutiérrez's observation that, whereas much contemporary theology seeks to respond to the challenge of the "nonbeliever" who questions our "religious world" as Christians, in a continent like Latin America the primary challenge comes to us rather from the "nonperson" who questions us about our "economic, social, political and cultural world."

The more I have reflected on this observation, the more I have come to believe that the category of "nonperson" is indefinitely more appropriate than that of "nonbeliever" for identifying the one whose questions an adequate theology must seek to answer. If by "nonperson" is meant one who, being excluded from the existing order in one or more respects, is to that extent unfree, a passive object of history instead of its active subject, then even the nonbeliever is a nonperson with respect to the existing religious order. On the other hand, since the nonbeliever is by no means the only person excluded from the social and political order in which the traditional witness of faith is implicated, to think of theology as having to give answer to the questions of the nonperson is more likely to take account of all those to whom theology owes a serious response.

The Faith That Works by Love

Beyond this, Gutiérrez's observation, along with converging insights of other liberation theologians, has led me to realize that the ideology involved in the traditional formulations of faith's claims is as much a problem as the mythology they involve in establishing their credibility to contemporary men and women. Positively or negatively, intentionally or unintentionally, the traditional witness of faith has served again and again to justify the interests of one group of human beings against those of others—whether class, nation, race or gender.

Because this is so, I have come to see an important, if rather obvious, parallel to Rudolf Bultmann's solution to the contemporary theological problem, which has long been decisive for my thinking. Just as in Bultmann's analysis the questions of belief and truth that theology now faces can be adequately answered only by way of radical demythologizing and existentialist interpretation, so it is now clear to me that what is required if theology is to deal satisfactorily with the issues of action and justice (which for many persons are even more urgent) is a theological method comprising thoroughgoing de-ideologizing and political interpretation.

Nor is this the end of the parallel. For if Bultmann's final defense of an existentialist theology is not that it is apologetically imperative, but that it is, with respect to belief, the contemporary expression of the Pauline doctrine that we are justified by faith alone without the words of the law, it seems to me that the final and comparably sufficient defense of a liberation theology is that it is, with respect to action, the contemporary expression of the equally Pauline doctrine that the only faith that justifies is the faith that works by love.

There is no question, then, that my mind has changed as I have tried to come to terms with the theologies for which I am prepared to offer such a defense—whether black theologies or women's theologies or the theologies emerging from Latin America and other sectors of the Third World. Although my response to their challenge has hardly been uncritical, I remain profoundly grateful to them for the help they have given me and any number of my students in more adequately understanding our own theological responsibility. On this score, suffice it to add only that if a resurgent fundamentalism confirms that the truth of the Christian witness continues to be a problem for theology as well as the church, the support currently being shown by Christians for the reactionary politics of the New Right makes only too clear that the same is true of the justice of their witness as well.

The Question of the Christian Norm

Important as it is, however, this change has been along lines familiar to me from my background in liberal theology, including the tradition of the social gospel, and thus is a matter of deepening and broadening my thinking more than of substantially revising it. But if this is true even of this first change, it is truer still of the only other development in my recent thinking that I take to be of comparable importance.

Up to this point, I have spoken of theology's concern with the credibility of the Christian witness, which concern arises from the fact that Christian faith itself claims to be credible in terms of common human experience. In this connection, I have acknowledged my new sense that there is a practical as well as a theoretical aspect to such credibility, and that theology must concern itself with the justice of the Christian witness as well as the truth of that witness if it is to vindicate the Christian claim.

But as crucial as this concern with credibility seems for any fully adequate theology, I am as little inclined now as I have been all along to suppose that it could ever be theology's only concern. Equally essential is that theology concern itself with the appropriateness of the Christian witness, by which I mean the congruence of what is meant in this witness, however it may be said, with what is properly taken to be the Christian norm. But this raises the question of just what *is* properly taken to be the Christian norm, and as I have continued to think about this question, it has become increasingly clear to me why I can no longer answer it as I did a decade ago.

Actually, the turning point came in spring 1974, during a seminar on the authority of Scripture for theology. Like many other Protestant theologians of my generation, I had been led early in my studies to accept the understanding of Scripture typical of neo-orthodoxy. In this understanding, one distinguishes between the Bible itself and the so-called biblical message contained within it, which is taken to be the real source of the Bible's authority. Thus my answer to the question of the Christian norm, by which the appropriateness of the Christian witness is to be judged, had come to be Scripture, especially the New Testament, understood in terms of its own essential witness. As a result of my reading and reflection during that seminar, however, I reached the conclusion that this answer is untenable. The reasoning that seemed—and still seems—to compel this conclusion goes as follows.

The Criterion of Canonicity

Formally considered, there are two possibilities for making the neo-orthodox distinction between the canon of Scripture itself and "the canon within the canon" of the scriptural witness, depending on whether one does or does not presuppose the first in determining the second. If one does not presuppose the canon, one's determination of the scriptural witness is open to the charge either of being arbitrary or of depending on some authority outside the scriptural witness that is one's real norm for judging.

If, on the contrary, one does presuppose the canon in determining the scriptural witness, one is faced with the objection that the writings of Scripture or of the New Testament can no longer be assumed to constitute a proper canon. This objection rests on the claim that, given our present historical methods and knowledge, none of the writings of

Scripture as such can be held to satisfy the early church's own criteria of canonicity.

We now know not only that none of the Old Testament writings is *prophetic* witness to Christ in the sense in which the early church assumed them to be, but also that none of the writings of the New Testament is *apostolic* witness to Christ as the early church itself understood apostolicity. The sufficient evidence of this point in the case of the New Testament writings is that all of them have now been shown to depend on sources, written or oral, earlier than themselves, and hence not to be the original and originating witness that the early church mistook them to be in judging them to be apostolic.

But this means, then, that one cannot accept the methods and findings of a historical critical understanding of Scripture while still maintaining the traditional Protestant scriptural principle, even in the revisionary form in which neo-orthodoxy continued to uphold it. Given what historians and exegetes now generally take for granted about the composition of the New Testament, the distinction between "Scripture" and "tradition" breaks down; and one is forced to decide either for a traditional New Testament canon that one can no longer justify by the early church's own criterion of apostolicity or else for this same criterion of canonicity that now allows one to justify only a nontraditional canon.

I must say that once this choice became clear to me, I was never in doubt how to make it. To me it has long seemed to belong to the very constitution of Christian existence that all appropriately Christian faith and witness are and must be apostolic. If one exists as a Christian at all, either one *is* an apostle, in the strict sense of being an original and originating witness to Jesus Christ, or else one believes and bears witness *with* the apostles, solely on the basis of their prior faith and witness. But this is to say that there is nothing in the least wrong with the early church's criterion of canonicity, however mistaken its historical judgments in applying this criterion. On the contrary, the witness of the apostles is still rightly taken to be the real Christian norm, even if we today have to locate this norm not in the writings of the New Testament but in the earliest stratum of Christian witness accessible to us, given our own methods of historical analysis and reconstruction.

The Source of Christian Witness

As for just where we should locate the apostolic witness, I have nothing to add to the proposal of Willi Marxsen. In thinking about this whole matter of the canon, as about other related matters, I find myself greatly indebted to him. Marxsen argues—in my opinion, convincingly—that the real Christian norm is the witness to Jesus that makes up the earliest layer of the synoptic tradition. This so-called Jesus-kerygma, which is very definitely Christian witness even though its christology is merely implicit, in contrast with the explicit christology of the Christ-kerygma that we find in Paul and John and the other New Testament writings, represents the earliest witness of faith that we today are in a position to recover. Therefore, it is here, if anywhere—in what Marxsen sometimes speaks of as "the canon *before* the canon"—that we must now locate the witness of the apostles that abides as the real Christian norm.

This proposal implies, of course, that Scripture is the sole primary *source* of Christian witness rather than its sole primary *norm*, and that the first step one must take in using it as a theological authority is historical rather than hermeneutical. Specifically, that is the step of reconstructing the history of tradition, of which the first three Gospels are the documentation, so as thereby to identify the earliest stratum in this tradition, which is the real Christian canon by which even Scripture has whatever authority it has.

But there seems little reason to doubt that this kind of reconstruction can be successfully carried out. The procedures required to execute it are identical with those long since worked out in the quest of the historical Jesus—with the single, if crucial, difference that in this case there is no need to make any dubious inferences about Jesus himself, once the earliest stratum of Christian witness has been reconstructed. Consequently, if one believes it possible to find the historical Jesus, one may be quite confident of finding what we today can rightly take to be the apostolic witness and hence the proper canon for judging the appropriateness of all Christian witness and theology.

These are the two changes, then, that I myself take to be most important as I review the course of my recent theological thinking. Perhaps now that I have described them, the reader will better understand why, in my own analysis, neither involves an abrupt discontinuity with my earlier life and thought, even though each has made for a different and, I should hope, more adequate understanding.

In any event, I find that I have begun the decade of the '80s still firmly committed to the same essential project with which I entered the '60s: to work toward a genuinely postliberal theology that, being sensitive at once to the human concern for freedom and to the claims of Christian faith, will be as concerned for the credibility of the church's witness when judged in terms of changing human experience as for the appropriateness of its witness when judged by reference to its abiding apostolic norm.

JÜRGEN MOLTMANN

The Challenge of Religion in the '80s

History doesn't depend on dates. Nor does it parcel itself out in decades, each with a neat label for easy identification. Talk about "the '60s," "the '70s" or "the '80s" doesn't even come close to an understanding of the actual experience of history. Nevertheless, people depend on dates—to order history and to organize events. And we stop at the end of a decade to take stock, to ask: How did we get here? Where do we go from here?

Our evaluation of the events of the past ten years is irrevocably influenced by which side of the fence we were on in the '60s. But no matter which side people were on, they describe that decade in ways that are remarkably similar. After the outbreak of hope, after the awakening of new life styles in almost every area of life in the years following 1960, after the decade of promise and possibility, we met in the oil crisis of 1973 an impossibility which we could not ignore.

A World with Limits

With that shock it became suddenly and sharply clear—if only for a moment—that we live no longer in a "world of unlimited possibilities," but rather in a situation in which we are cornered by increasing shortages and scarcity on all sides. The revolutionary '60s were followed by the reactionary '70s. The outbreak of hope ran head-on into opposition, resistance and doubt. Worldwide protest was replaced by common retreat into self-pity. The cult of the individual and the individual's rights ruled the '70s. Not Prometheus but Narcissus was the idol of this era.

In 1978 the news analysts of *Time* magazine announced as the chief characteristic of the Germans not their acclaimed workaholism, nor their economic miracle, but their anxiety. That anxiety should be the controlling mood of people in an economically successful country is not only remarkable—it is dangerous. Anxiety breeds aggression. It extorts and distorts. It shrouds the future in shadow. Will we learn to live with this anxiety? How will we overcome it so that we can accomplish undaunted what we have to do before it is too late? This, it seems to me, is the question of the '80s.

If we look at the religious landscape of the '70s, then we must acknowledge—whether we want to or not—that the challenge of secularization to Christianity has disappeared. Christianity is now challenged by a revitalization of religion. Those critics of the church who had reckoned with a "death of religion" (Marx, Lenin) miscalculated. Those who had hoped for a "religionless Christianity" (Bonhoeffer) were disappointed. Those who proclaimed that "God is dead" now learn to fear the god of Ayatollah Khomeini.

The Search for Religious Experience

There is a strong tendency in the secular world view to demand the sacrifice of all other religious drives to its own belief in progress. But the more the secular belief in progress—be it capitalistic, socialistic or positivistic—thrives on the crises it creates for itself, the more strongly do religious passions surface in public life. Politically, the modern underestimation of religion has led to mistaken judgments that have critical consequences—for example, Washington's inability to understand the recent events in Iran.

When we ask which discussions have disappeared from theological debate, we are confronted with a similar series of events. The secularization debate, the remythologization discussion, the "God is dead" theology, and the questions of religion's critics—Feuerbach, Marx, Freud and Nietzsche—are obsolete. They have been replaced by so-called religious topics, from meditation to the myths and stories of people to the organization of religion.

The new search for religious experience is deeply ambiguous. Religious experience is as much a challenge to the Christian faith as is secularization. If the religious phenomena we experience today witness to anything, it is to the profound truth of Berdyaev: "Man is incurably religious." Religion is thus as much a threat as a hope. "Religious" people can become the most dangerous on earth. The Christian faith cannot choose to distance itself from religion. But neither can it identify itself with religion. The Christian faith must bring its healing and liberating power to these various religious phenomena. In my book *The Crucified God* (Harper & Row, 1974) I tried to argue that faith in the crucified

Christ is the faith that heals and frees us. In Christendom everything must be tested by the cross, secularity as well as religion.

Today the challenge of religion meets us *in* the churches and, even more, *through* the churches. Here it pulls us in two opposite directions at the same time. We hear it in the call for security, authority and belonging. But we hear it also in the cry for more freedom, spontaneity and community. Consequently, we find a powerful polarization. On one hand, the Christian church moves toward the bureaucracy of an organized religion; on the other, it moves toward the spirit of a voluntary community.

The Church in Tension

After the fall of the state church in 1919, the Protestant church in Germany saw itself as a people's church (*Volkskirche*). The church was for everyone; it was open to everyone—but only for their religious needs. The *Volkskirche* is a church *for* the people, not *of* and *by* the people. By definition, the people's church stands above political parties and social conflicts. The church presents itself as the third party in mediation and reconciliation. It takes no political stance. One-sided partisan and critical statements violate the church's social constitution.

The contemporary critic of religion has protested vehemently against this posture. But the '70s' answer to the church critics of the '60s was the attempt totally to assimilate church and society in the name of organized religion. The church should satisfy the religious needs of people in the society; it should trust, advise and lead the people; it should protect the society with a religious network of spiritual security. The church should release people from deciding for themselves about moral and religious principles; it should organize the meaning of life for them, and assure them of the higher values of their society.

Prerequisite for all of this, of course, is that everybody "belong" to the church. Active participation is not required, or even wished.

This is the explanation for the curious situation in Germany, where 95 per cent of the people "belong" to a church, only 10–15 per cent participate actively, and the church is nonetheless considered to be fairly "stable." If Christians give in to this tendency, they will one day discover that their religion is only circumstantially related to Christianity. The Christian faith would then become unnecessary and dispensable.

On the other side, there is the movement toward spontaneity and the growth of autonomous communities. During the recent annual celebration in West Germany of Protestant and Roman Catholic church days (*Kirchentage*), the full-blown impact of this movement became more and more apparent. The hall with the "Market of Alternatives" in the Nuremberg festival displayed not 100 but 1,000 different varieties of community and styles of spontaneity. There were core communities and diakonia communities, therapeutic, social, political, academic, proletariat, charismatic, ecumenical, missionary and feminist communities scattered throughout. Each offered its own alternative to established religion: voluntary commitment, comprehensive community, liberating self-realization.

We can believe only what we ourselves have experienced and understood. We can be held responsible only for what we have decided according to our own consciences. We can experience the church only when we experience the community in which all people are free because they accept one another and throw all cultural prejudices to the wind. Here we can be spontaneous. Here we can live concretely. Here we can do something practical. "Established norms and values" and "unquestioned recognition of authority" have nothing to do with real life.

If one asks these Christians how their faith and their inner lives are nurtured, they answer: first, through the voluntary character of the community, and second, in the concrete experience of the community. The institutional church has been left lying in the dust. In my book *The Church in the Power of the Spirit* (Harper & Row, 1977), I suggested theologically responsible and practical steps toward a conversion of the "people's church" into a community church. I see myself as a "free-church person" in the midst of a *Volkskirche*.

The "Youth Religions"

The churches in West Germany are losing their monopoly on religion in these decades. This development is a second religious challenge. The pluralism of voluntary, autonomous communities is also ambiguous. More and more frequently missionaries and religious agitators surface who speak of the "church" in terms of churches. The most notorious of these groups is the Unification Church of the Korean Sun Myung Moon—the Moonies. Their doctrine is a simplistic messianism; their organization, tactics and strategy, however, are highly sophisticated. We are accustomed to lumping this and other meditative and occult practices together under the label "new religions." Many people call them "youth religions" (*Jugendreligionen*).

But in fact the Christian churches in Europe stand powerless before these new phenomena. They feel threatened by Hare Krishna, Mun Bagwan and others, and they react to them as the privileged churches, the churches of kings and popes, have always reacted against heretics. The sweet seduction of the youth religions—with their escape into an ersatz family structure, their spiritual retreat to a security that demands no responsibility, their blind obedience to authority—is life-threatening.

On one hand, these new religions are temptations for young people and old to step out of a life which they fear they cannot deal with. On the other hand, such groups offer healing for people suffering in the technocratic society. Whoever has experienced the "inner light" knows that he or she is not a nobody. One steps out of anonymity and powerlessness. Whoever comes before the bureaucratic tangle of society, like Kafka's defendant in *The Trial*, finds in these religious communities a "family": one knows that one "belongs."

These new religions succeed precisely because of the deficiencies and contradictions which the church and the society have created and cannot seem to overcome. They point to what is wrong and sick in the relationship between church and society. Finally, the new religious underground reveals the guilty conscience of church and society. So long as these two stay as they are, these new underground religions will continue to expand. A single, uniform and controlled religious world can never be reinstated through sanction and censure.

"Strangers in Their Own Country"

If the church loses its monopoly on religion in society, it also loses its claim to be the single representative of Christianity. For this reason, many of the above-mentioned voluntary groups and basic communities offer a variety of options and alternatives for believers. The more immobile and conservative the church superstructure becomes, the more seriously the Christian action and movement of these groups must be taken. These groups can move freely and decisively.

Implicitly, a "people's church" will always represent the ruling interests of its own people; a civil religion openly represents the interests of the groups in power. Only voluntary and determined groups, made up of people who are prepared to become "strangers in their own country," can operate against the prevailing interests and the pressure of self-interested parties. This was the experience of the Confessing Church in the struggle during the Nazi regime (*Kirchenkampf*). It is also the experience of the church in South Africa, South Korea, Latin America.

The more Christians in West Germany come into ecumenical solidarity with the peoples of the Third World, the more they come into conflict with the established loyalties of their own people. And they are often left in the lurch by church leaders who have to move cautiously in order not to offend anyone. This was the bitter experience not only of the student congregations but also of the Protestant churchwomen who organized to boycott fruit from South Africa. If our churches surrender to the values and interests of the Bundesrepublik, they will be alienated from ecumenical community with the churches in the Third World. In the case of black liberation movements in southern Africa and Latin American liberation theology, a new "Babylonian captivity" of the church appears. This is no accusation; it is rather a statement of fact.

From this it follows that necessary Christian actions and movements must be taken over more and more by groups and movements within the church, rather than by the church itself. To what extent can the church integrate these various groups? When must separations be taken into account? Over what issues? To be able to make such determinations presupposes an understanding of what is distinctively Christian. But without such an understanding, and without faith, the church cannot answer the religious challenge.

Foresight and wish are mingled together in every projection for the '80s. This projection is no exception: it is unabashedly personal. After the outbreak of hope in the '60s in which I participated, and after the experience of anxiety and the retreat into the self, which I suffered rather unwillingly during the '70s, I see in the future neither a new euphoria of hope nor widespread panic. I see rather the beginnings of a sober heroism.

By that I mean courage in the midst of legitimate anxiety, caution in the midst of mobilized hope. I mean the courage to do what we have to do decisively before it is too late. We need hope which is made wise by experience but is undaunted by disappointment. We need an anxiety about the future that teaches us new self-consciousness but does not unnerve us. Many people full of hope wrecked themselves on the problems of the world, because they couldn't handle themselves. Others left the world in an attempt to find themselves. Both roads lead to dead ends. In the future we must approach the real problems of the world without self-contempt, and we must find self-assurance without pessimism.

DAVID TRACY

Defending the Public Character of Theology

For the past ten years, three theological issues have concerned me most: the public nature of theology, the religious reality of fundamental trust, and the meaning of theological pluralism.

The issue of the public nature of theology is a familiar one. The shorthand word for the cultural problem which this question of publicness addresses is the "privatization of religion." A major concern for any religious thinker is that religion often serves as another purely private option with merely private effects. Yet no major religion, properly understood, can accept a privatistic self-understanding. Indeed, theologians of every radically monotheistic religion realize that its fundamental commitment to God demands that we express that theistic belief in ways that will render it public not merely to ourselves or our particular religious group. No Christian or Jewish theologian alert to the radical theocentrism at the heart of theology can rest content with the fatal social view that religious convictions are purely "personal preferences" or "private options."

The Thrust to Publicness

If a theologian does rest content with privateness, no one in our society will really mind. There are many "reservations of the spirit" for the weary in American society. One more will not prove too burdensome. But whenever a theologian will not allow a societal definition of religion as a sometimes useful, sometimes dangerous, usually harmless "private option," then the struggle of contemporary theology for authentic publicness begins. If theologians in the liberal tradition, moreover, resign themselves to privateness, they unwittingly betray the genius of that tradition. They also reject the heart of that tradition's attempt to achieve publicness through persuasive argument. Indeed, they hand over that public role of theology to the coercive tactics of a resurgent reaction announcing itself as the "Moral Majority."

It is not, of course, the case that all theologians should accept an explicit concern with "publicness" as their major focus. A thrust to publicness must, however, be present in all theologies. Otherwise, theo-logy no longer exists. Such is my conviction. It is a conviction based on the theological warrant that any seriously theocentric construal of reality demands publicness. To speak and mean God-language is to speak publicly and mean it. Theologians must speak of many matters. And yet, if they are not also speaking of God while they address these other issues, they are not doing theology. Theologians can and must speak in many forms and genres. But if they are not articulating a public position, they are not speaking theologically.

To speak in a public fashion means to speak in a manner that can be disclosive and transformative for any intelligent, reasonable, responsible human being. Yet how is that ideal actualized in theology? First, theologians must pay more attention to the primary social realities (the actual "publics") informing every particular theology. Second, theologians must argue how the general "publicness" of all theological language is actualized into distinct but related theological disciplines. A good deal of my own theological reflection in the past ten years has been the attempt to speak to these two interrelated dimensions of the single issue of the public character of theology.

The battle for historical consciousness in theology has been waged for over 150 years. In the present climate of a neoconservative resurgence in both the churches and society, that cause may be endangered in some theological circles. Even so, the fight for historical consciousness in mainline theologies seems basically secure. For myself, certain early formative influences in the early '60s (biblical criticism, Bernard Lonergan's reflections on method and historical consciousness, and the splendid ambience of student days in Rome during the Second Vatican Council) solidified my own sharing in the common conviction that there can be no return to a pre-ecumenical, prepluralistic, ahistorical theology. Historical consciousness may be rejected at the moment by some official church authorities. Yet that consciousness and all it implies for theology cannot be rejected by theologians. And it will not be rejected by history itself.

More recently, a social-scientific consciousness has also entered theology, with effects both as disturbing and as liberating as theology's earlier recognition of the need for historical consciousness. Indeed, a "sociological imagination" is slowly transforming all theologies—sometimes with unsettling and explicit power, as in the use of critical social theories in political and liberation theologies; sometimes with more implicit but no less unsettling effect, as in the increasing use of sociology of knowledge to clarify the actual social settings (or publics) of different theologies.

The use of social science suggests that the question of the public character of theology is best posed first, as noted above, as a question of these different publics to which theologies are addressed. For the kinds of "publicness" achieved by different theologies are strongly influenced by the distinct kinds of social realities (or publics) from which theologies emerge and to which they speak. As a discipline, theology has the peculiarity of being related to three distinct publics—academy, church and society. Any genuine theological proposal that really means what it says about God implicitly addresses all three publics.

In fact, however, most theologies emerge from and are principally addressed to one of these three publics. Academic theologies (with their focus on such questions as method, the disciplinary status of theology in the modern university, the relationships of theology and religious studies, and the development of public criteria for theological language) are obviously related principally to the public of the academy. Many other theologies are more explicitly church-related in both their principal interests and their primary audience. Still other theologies are far more concerned with a theological response to societal struggles for justice. In every case the primary social locus (or "public") of the theologian (society, academy, church) will undoubtedly influence but need not determine the particular form of public theological criteria and language that are used.

Breaking Through the Swamp of Privateness

This is not to say that theology should now become social science. Indeed, as Harnack correctly observed of historical study itself, history (and, we can now add, social science) must have the first word in theology but cannot have the last. There an explicitly theological analysis must occur. For all theologies intend their language to include a fully public character. All theologies are implicitly related to all three publics even though usually one public (society, academy or church) will be primary.

My own proposal on particular ways through which publicness occurs is to argue that there exist three major subdisciplines constituting theology—viz., fundamental, systematic and practical theology. This proposal is easy enough to state briefly yet impossible to defend short of lengthy analysis and argument.

In an attempt to provide those necessary arguments, I have written two related books: first, a book on fundamental theology (*Blessed Rage for Order: The New Pluralism in Theology* [Seabury, 1975]). That book defends the first and obvious meaning of publicness (viz., as meaning and truth available to all intelligent, reasonable and rational persons through persuasive argument) for the logically ordered questions of religion, God and Christ. A recently completed book on systematic theology (*The Analogical Imagination: Christian Theology and the Culture of Pluralism* [Crossroad, 1981]) defends a second, less obvious but no less genuine notion of the kind of publicness that systematic theologies actually achieve.

I continue to believe that the discipline of fundamental theology is necessary to investigate critically the central claims of Christianity. I continue to believe that this kind of enterprise is indeed fundamental for the attempt to break through the swamp of privateness that afflicts religion and theology in our day. The basic strategy of that earlier book still seems correct to me: an attempt to develop criteria of publicness for responding to the three central questions posed to Christian belief. First, is a religious interpretation of our common human experience meaningful and true? Second, is a belief in God as the proper referent of that religious experience and language meaningful and true? Third, within that religious and theistic frame of reference, is it meaningful to appeal to the particularity of the Christian event of Jesus Christ?

I suspect that the way the questions are posed already suggests that my basic response to each of these questions is affirmative, as indeed it is. My public warrants for a Yes to religion, God and Christ are articulated in that book on fundamental theology. Since I have not in fact "changed my mind" in any basic way on the availability of a positive response to all three questions, I will here move on to the more difficult question of the public nature of systematic theologies. Here some important changes have occurred for me.

Appeals to Particularity

At first sight, it seems counterintuitive to suggest that systematic theologies are public. For systematic theologies, after all, are theological expressions of a particular religious tradition's construal of all reality from the vantage point of that religious particularity. Moreover, the ease with which Christian theologians can move from an emphasis on Christian particularity to the trap of Christian exclusivism (especially in Christology for Protestants, in ecclesiology for Catholics) has made me wary of many theological appeals to particularity. Are not these appeals to particularity often sophisticated expressions of a private option from the fabled land of personal preferences? And yet this correct suspicion clashes with another basic intuition: the greatest works of art and all the major religions are in fact highly particular in both origin and expression.

Every classic work of art reaches public (and sometimes universal) status through, not despite, its particularity. All the major religions remain deeply rooted in highly particular experiences, persons, events, rituals, symbols. Religions tend to collapse as religions whenever their rootedness in particularity is ripped away by later reflection. Each of us contributes more to the common good when we dare to undertake a journey into our own particularity (this family, this community, this people, this culture, this religion) than when we attempt to homogenize all differences in favor of some lowest common denominator. Like the ancient Romans who made a desert and called it peace, we are tempted to root out all particularity and call it publicness.

A full defense of this intuition as true (i.e., as "public") demands the kind of argument and modes of reflection which I have attempted in my recently completed work on systematic theology (*The Analogical Imagination*). Pursuing that intuition in research for four years proved, for me at least, liberating. When I wrote *Blessed Rage for Order*, I did state that even if the arguments for the public character of fundamental theology in that book were sound, those arguments could not determine the distinctive form of publicness proper to systematic theology or that proper to practical theology. At that time (1975) I knew that there was a real difference between fundamental and systematic theology and, therefore, between the forms of publicness proper to each. Yet I could not then formulate exactly what the difference was.

A Theory of the Classic

The central puzzle became the paradox of the classic. The initial paradox I formulated this way: Why do the classic systematic theologies, like the classic works of art, function so disclosively, indeed so publicly, in spite of their particularity? The most important change of mind I have experienced has been the gradual replacement of that crucial "in spite of" clause with a firm "because of." The productive paradox of the classic is that every classic in both art and religion achieves its genuine publicness because of, not in spite of, an intensified particularity.

To understand this productive paradox, I turned first to the experience of art and developed a theory of "the classic." This theory provides an argument for how the experience of a public disclosure of truth actually happens in the classic works of art. I then reflected upon the distinctive characteristics of the religious classic and, more specifically, the Christian classic: the person and event of Jesus Christ.

I attempted, therefore, to develop public criteria for the truth of art and religion as distinct but related disclosures of truth (for systematic theology). I am now attempting to develop public criteria of ethical (personal and societal) transformation for practical theology. A book on practical theology now preoccupies me in the same way that an earlier struggle for public criteria in fundamental theology concerned me in the early '70s and the struggle for criteria of meaning and truth in the disclosures of the beautiful and the holy in the classic works of art and religion preoccupied me in the late '70s. Such was—and is—the basic program designed to defend the public character of theology. Whether that program succeeds or fails, the readers (i.e., the public) must finally decide.

Of this much, however, I feel sure: no theologian can long avoid these kinds of issues if the character of theology as serious speech about God is to survive. A culture can abandon metaphysics, marginalize art, and privatize religion—but it will eventually pay a heavy price. Our increasingly splintered society has begun to recognize how heavy the price can be. Consider the disturbing witness of our present American spectacle: a popular and privatistic gospel of self-fulfillment lined up against the deceptively "public" gospel of the "Moral Majority." Can these really be our only choices: the pathos of privateness or coercive theological nonsense? For ethicists, philosophers, artists and theologians, both alternatives should be unacceptable.

The Universality of the Divine Reality

As these reflections on the public character of theology indicate, my own major social locus is the academy—more exactly, for the past ten years, that remarkable center of colleagueship and scholarship, the University of Chicago divinity school. I recognize that my theology bears all the marks (including the negative ones) of what many now criticize as "academic theology." Yet I can see no good reason, short of abandoning my own particularity, for forsaking those limitations and those possibilities. Each theologian, to repeat, is related implicitly to all three publics. I have been fortunate enough to be explicitly related to all three. Yet whether our relationships to academy, society or church are implicit or explicit, we all must remind ourselves anew of certain theological realities in our present situation.

Each theologian attempts to speak in and to three publics. The demands and the plausibility-structures of each public have been internalized to different degrees of radicality in each theologian. That drive to publicness which constitutes all good theological discourse is a drive from and to those three publics. Existentially, the theologian invests loyalty and trust in both church and world. Each strives, as a single self, to recognize that one's fundamental faith and loyalty are to God. Each knows, as a theological interpreter of Christian self-understanding, that faith in God includes a fundamental trust in and loyalty to both church and world. We know that only God is an unambiguous object of loyalty and trust. We also know that both church and world are as ambiguous in actuality as the internal conflicts in the "foul rag and bone shop of the heart." To live with that ambiguity is incumbent upon every Christian. To try to think honestly, critically and clearly in relationship to it is incumbent upon every theologian.

Many theologians try to resolve this dilemma by choosing one of the three publics as their primary reference group. They tend to leave the other two publics at the margins of their consciousness.

Theologians also recognize, however, that their fundamental trust and loyalty are to the all-pervasive reality of God. Any radically monotheistic understanding of the reality of God (whether classical, process, liberationist or liberal) affirms the strict universality of the divine reality. Whatever else it is, any Christian theology is ultimately and radically theocentric. An insight into the universal character of the divine reality as the always-present object of the Christian's trust and loyalty is what ultimately impels every theology to attempt publicness. For God as understood by the Jew or Christian is either universal in reality or sheer delusion. Theology in all its forms is finally nothing else but the attempt to reflect deliberately and critically upon that reality. Theology is *logos* on *theos*.

A theologian's private universality is, at best, an oxymoron. At worst it is a serious misunderstanding of the fundamental reality of God. If faith in God is serious, then any discourse about that faith must be public. An understanding of the reality of God ultimately should determine all other theological discourse, just as fundamental trust in and loyalty to God should determine all one's other loyalties.

An Ambiguous World

Theologians also acknowledge the ambiguous reality of all three publics. *A public of a society* where reason is often reduced to sheer instrumentality, where technology is in danger of becoming technocracy—yet a public where the interest of a genuine public good is symbolically, legally and politically affirmed and where a "rough justice" can occasionally prevail. *A public of the academy* where too often Plato is preached while Hobbes is practiced, yet where the interests of critical reason and civilized experience are honored and practiced even in the breach. *A public of the church* where the bureaucrat finds new "outlets" for "input," where mystification and repression can often breathe heavily—yet still a public where the gift of God's liberating word is preached, where the sacraments of God's encompassing reality are re-presented, where the dangerous memory of Jesus is kept alive, where a genuine community of persons who actually live the Christian reality may yet be found.

Does it not follow that the theologian should maintain trust in and loyalty to all three publics as concrete expressions of "world" and "church" so long as loyalty to God remains the first and pervasive loyalty?

In an ambiguous world, an ambiguous self can still find trust. In a broken world where the sense of the reality of the whole often discloses itself as a sense of the eclipse of the reality of God, one can still find a fundamental trust in the very meaningfulness of existence itself. Thereby can we learn anew to trust in the reality Jews and Christians name God. If that trust is articulated in the properly eschatological terms of Christian self-understanding, then a confident hope for a future full recognition of that God, a hope for a vision of the whole beyond present ambiguity and brokenness, is disclosed in the proleptic manifestation called Jesus Christ. A gift that is also a command; an enigma that is also a promise; an ambiguity that is also an assurance—in such terms does the Christian consciousness attempt to understand both itself and the encompassing reality.

Yet as important as such methodological reflections on the public character of theology may be, they should not become the occasion to shirk reflection on the central issues of theology. As Karl Rahner rightly remarks, "We cannot spend all our time sharpening the knife; at some point we must cut." Such theological cutting as I have done has centered on three central theological doctrines: the nature of religion (and, therefore, of revelation), the nature of God, and, more recently, the nature of Christology. I have tried to speak on these three issues in the books cited and shall try to speak on them again and more adequately in the future. My positions on all three are probably still best described as revisionary (i.e., the use of a "limit-language" approach to the questions of religion and revelation; the use of process categories for understanding the reality of God; and the use of symbolic literary-critical analyses for interpreting Christology).

A Route Highlighting the Negative

Upon reflection, I cannot claim that any major changes on the issues of religion, God or Christ have occurred for me over the past ten years. Still, I do hope that my more recent work develops the sometimes fairly embryonic positions (especially on Christology) presented in *Blessed Rage for Order.*

On one substantive issue, however, I do think that I have experienced something like a sea-change in both sensibility and theological understanding. In my earlier work, I tended to emphasize an approach to religion by means of reflection upon what can be called the positive limit-experiences of life. I especially emphasized the experience of fundamental trust as the principal contemporary "secular" clue for approaching the meaning of religion, God and Christ.

I do not doubt that fundamental trust remains a crucial (and still widely overlooked) phenomenon for approaching the issues of religion and God. Yet I have come to doubt that the route from fundamental trust to religion and God can prove as direct or as unencumbered as I once thought. More exactly, I no longer believe that the "route" of the negative realities (anxiety, responsible guilt, death, illness, bereavement, alienation and oppression) is correctly described as an alternative route to the questions of religion and God.

Rather, the profound negativities of human existence—personal, societal and historical—seem so pervasive in this age that any route to fundamental trust must be far more circuitous, tentative and even potholed than I had once hoped. The Christian symbols that speak to those realities of negation—cross, apocalyptic, sin, the demonic, the radically incomprehensible, the hidden and revealed God—strike home to me today far more than they ever did before.

The theological results, as I suspect my recent work shows, are clear enough. My theological understandings of religion, God and Jesus Christ remain fundamentally the same in substance yet really different in tone. For the route to those interpretations is now arrived at less quickly and even less surely. The experience of fundamental trust remains as central to me as it ever was. Yet even that trust has now become subtly transformed by being arrived at only through a route highlighting the negative at every moment of the theological journey.

The classic theological language of analogy (the language of somehow ordered relationships) remains my real theological home. Yet now the analogies emerge more tentatively through (not in spite of) the various languages of radical negative dialectics. This recognition of the need for both the negative and the positive as always already together in every religious journey has forced me onto a more unsteady route for every question of theology.

The Darker Side of Pluralism

I have never, for example, regretted or bemoaned contemporary theological pluralism. I have always assumed that any authentic pluralism—personal, cultural, theological, religious—is an enrichment, not an impoverishment, of the human spirit. I still trust my instinctive affirmation of our pluralistic actuality.

Yet I have come to see more clearly the darker side of this pluralistic vision. Whenever pluralism slides into the all-too-human option of a simpleminded "let a thousand flowers bloom," it corrodes even as it builds. Whenever pluralism becomes too content with a relaxed model of "dialogue," it can ignore the need for conflict and the actualities of systematic distortions in the personal (psychosis), historical (alienation and oppression) and religious (sin) dimensions of every person, culture and tradition. Whenever pluralism in theology resists the need for argument, warrants, theory, evidence, praxis, it becomes a kind of Will Rogers pluralism: one where theologians have never met a position they didn't like. I have met several I didn't like. So, too, has every other responsible pluralist.

In order to continue a genuine affirmation of pluralism despite the profound negative realities in the buzzing, blooming confusion of this pluralistic moment, I have turned to a strategy I name "the analogical imagination." Technical matters on analogy aside for the moment, the strategy itself rests on certain basic beliefs. We understand one another, if at all, only through analogy. Who you are I know only if you will allow me to sense—through a gesture, a text, a symbol, a story, a theory, a way of life—what central vision of existence actually empowers your life. If we converse, we shall both be changed. For then our central visions will meet and conflict, join and depart, and, in that very dialectic, disclose the genuine differences, the latent negativities, the possible identities and, above all, the similarities-in-difference (the analogies) in every life and all thinking.

The global culture which the present suggests and the future demands impels everyone—every individual, every group, every culture, every religious and theological tradition—to recognize the plurality within each self, among all selves, all traditions, all cultures in the face of the elusive, pervasive whole of reality: the whole which Christian and Jew know as the Who named God. Our present situation demands that each come to the dialogue with a genuine self-respect in her or his particularity as well as a willingness to expose oneself as oneself to the other as really other. Self-exposure is merely the reverse side of the self-respect demanded by this pluralistic moment.

Authentic Conversation

To the neoconservatives of the moment, no such theological strategy for embracing pluralism without forfeiting mind, negativity, argument, rootedness, tradition, particularity can ever succeed. The neoconservative strategy for the '80s is quite different. All we need do, it seems, is return home and bolt the doors. All we can hope for is that our own particular reservation of the spirit will be the last to fall.

Yet the neoconservatives are in fact more "neo" than conserving. No tradition ever was or will be conserved by rejecting the enriching possibilities for change in the pluralistic reality of every historical moment. The now beleaguered non-neoconservatives in every tradition may find that something like an analogical imagination is at work among us all. The need—my need and theirs—is to find better ways in the future of articulating that imagination and that strategy in both theory and in practice.

Otherwise, the alternatives left to us seem bleak. Perhaps we should simply announce, with La Pasionara at the end of the Spanish Civil War,

"They took the cities, but we had better songs." It is a consoling thought. And we *do* have better songs. But the consolation is not necessarily what theology has to offer. It is time for the genuine pluralism among theologians to affirm itself again as a conversing, arguing, conflictual pluralism grounded in a common commitment to publicness. It is time to join in authentic conversation on the differences, the similarities-in-difference, the hidden and often repressed negativities in the communal task. It is time to forget the '70s and the consolations of our former songs and to try again to take the cities.

III

Interlude:
Literary Testimonies

ELIE WIESEL

Recalling Swallowed-Up Worlds

Have I changed? Of course. Everyone changes. To live means to traverse a certain time, a certain space: with a little luck, some traces are left. The traces at the beginning are not the same as those at the end. Certainly, my tradition teaches me that the road leads somewhere, and although the destination remains constant, the stages of the journey change and renew themselves. Attracted by childhood, the old man will seek it in a thousand different ways.

As in a Dusty Mirror

I am seeking my childhood; I will always be seeking it. I need it. It is necessary for me as a point of reference, as a refuge. It represents for me a world that no longer exists; a sunny and mysterious kingdom where beggars were princes in disguise, and fools were wise men freed from their constraints.

At that time, in that universe, everything seemed simple. People were born and died, hoped and despaired, invoked love or anguish as an invitation or a barrier. I understood certain things—not everything. I resigned myself to the idea that, for the essential experiences, the quest is itself a victory; even if it hardly succeeds, it represents a triumph. It was enough for me to know that someone knew the answer; what I myself sought was the question.

It was in this way that I viewed man and his place in creation: it was up to him to question what surrounded him and thus to go beyond himself. It is not by chance, I told myself, that the first question in the Bible is that which God puts to Adam: "Where are you?"

"What?" cried a great Hasidic master, Rabbi Shneour-Zalmen of Ladi. "God didn't know where Adam was? No, that's not the way to understand the question. God knew, Adam didn't."

That, I thought, is what one must always seek to know: one's role in society, one's place in history. It is one's duty to ask every day, "Where am I in relation to God and to others?"

And, strangely enough, the child knew what the adult would not. Yes, in my small town somewhere in the Carpathian Mountains, I knew where I was. I knew why I existed. I existed to glorify God and to sanctify his word. I existed to link my destiny to that of my people, and the destiny of my people to that of humanity. I existed to do good and to combat evil, to accomplish the will of heaven; in short, to fit each of my acts, each of my dreams, each of my prayers into God's design.

I knew that God was at the same time near and far, magnanimous and severe, rigorous and merciful. I knew that I belonged to his chosen people—people chosen to serve him by suffering as well as by hope. I knew that I was in exile and that the exile was total, universal, even cosmic. I knew as well that the exile would not last, that it would end in redemption. I knew so many things, about so many subjects. I knew especially when to rejoice and when to lament: I consulted the calendar; everything was there.

Now I no longer know anything.

As in a dusty mirror, I look at my childhood and I wonder if it is mine. I don't recognize myself in the child who studies there with fervor, who says his prayers. It's because he is surrounded by other children; he walks like them, with them, head bowed and lips tightened. He advances into the night as if attracted by its shadows. I watch them as they enter an abyss of flames, I see them transformed into ashes, I hear their cries turn into silence, and I no longer know anything; I no longer understand anything: they have taken away my certainties, and no one will give them back to me.

To Live in a Jewish World

It's not only a matter of questions concerning religious faith. It's a matter of those, too, and of all the others. It's a matter of redefining, or at least rethinking, my relations with others and with myself: have they changed? I think that I can answer Yes without the slightest hesitation. With perspective, I realize that they are no longer the same. Let me try to be more specific. My attitude toward Christians, for example: before the war, it was mistrustful if not hostile; after, open and hospitable.

Before the war, I avoided everyone who came from the other side—that is, from Christianity. Priests frightened me; I avoided them: so as not to pass them, I would cross the street. I dreaded all contact with them. I feared being kidnapped by them and baptized by force. I had heard so many rumors, so many stories of this type: I had the impression that I was always in danger.

At school, I sat with Christian boys of my age, but we didn't speak to one another. At recess we played separated by an invisible wall. I never visited a Christian schoolmate at home. We had nothing in common. Later, as an adolescent, I stayed away from them. I knew them to be capable of anything: of beating me, humiliating me by pulling my *payèss*, or seizing my skullcap, without which I felt naked. My dream back then? To live in a Jewish world, completely Jewish, a world where Christians would have scarcely any access. A protected world, ordered according to the laws of Sinai. It's strange, but awakening in the ghetto, I discovered in myself a feeling of exultation: after all, we were living among ourselves. I didn't yet know that it was only a step, the first, toward a small railroad station somewhere in Poland called Auschwitz.

Contrary to what I could think, my true change took place not in the camps, but after their liberation. During the ordeal, I lived in expectation: of a miracle or of death. Atrophied, I evolved passively, accepting events without questioning them. Certainly, I felt revolt and anger toward the murderers and their accomplices, and also toward the Creator who let them act as they did. I thought that humanity was lost forever and that God himself was not capable of saving it. I asked myself questions which formerly would have made me tremble: on the evil in man, on the silence of God. But I continued to act as though I still believed. Friendship in the camp was important to me; I looked for it despite the efforts of the killers to belittle and deny it. I clung to family ties despite the killers who changed them into dangerous, mortal traps. As for God, I continued to say my prayers. In the morning, I arose before the others to wait in line and put on the phylacteries.

A Time of Despair

It was only later, upon leaving the nightmare, that I underwent a prolonged crisis, painful and anguished, questioning my past certainties.

I began to despair of humanity and God; I considered them as enemies of one another, and both as enemies of the Jewish people. I didn't express this aloud, not even in my notes. I studied history, philosophy, psychology; I wanted to understand. The more I learned, the less I understood.

I was angry at the Germans: How could they have counted Goethe and Bach as their own and at the same time massacred countless Jewish children? I was angry at their Hungarian, Polish, Ukrainian, French and Dutch accomplices: How could they, in the name of a perverse ideology, have turned against their Jewish neighbors to the point of pillaging their houses and denouncing them? I was angry at Pope Pius XII: How could he have kept silent? I was angry at the heads of the Allied countries: How could they have given Hitler the impression that, as far as the Jews were concerned, he could do as he wished? Why hadn't they taken action to save them? Why had they closed all doors to them? Why hadn't they bombed the railroad line to Birkenau, if only to show Himmler that the Allies were not indifferent?

And—why not admit it?—I was angry at God too, at the God of Abraham, Isaac and Jacob: how could he have abandoned his people at the moment when they needed him? How could he have delivered them up to the killers? How could one explain, how could one justify the deaths of a million Jewish children?

For months and months, for years, I lived alone. I mistrusted my fellow humans; I suspected them. I no longer believed in the word as a vehicle of thought and of life; I shunned love, aspiring only to silence and madness. Disgusted with the West, I turned toward the East. I was attracted by Hindu mysticism; I was interested in Sufism; I even began to explore the occult domains of marginal sects here and there in Europe. It's simple: I was looking for something else. I was anxious to venture to the other side of reality, of what constituted the basis of civilization. Meditation counted more for me than action; I drowned myself in contemplation. The appearance of things repulsed me, that of people even more.

If I had been able to settle in an ashram somewhere in India, I would have. But I couldn't. I had seen, under the incandescent sky of India, an immeasurable, unnameable suffering. I couldn't bear it. In the face of this suffering, the problem of evil imposed itself on me with a destructive force. I could choose to steel myself to it or flee. Now I was not anxious to be an accomplice. Hindu friends would cross the street stepping over a crowd of mutilated and sick bodies without even looking at them. I couldn't. I looked and I felt guilty.

Finally I understood: I am free to choose my suffering but not that of my fellow humans. Not to see the hungry before me was to accept their destiny in their place, in their name, for them and even against them—or at least, like them. Not to notice their distress was to acquiesce to its logic, indeed to its justice. Not to cry out against their misery was to make it all the heavier. Because I felt myself too weak to cry out, to offer a hand to so many disfigured children, because I refused to understand that certain situations couldn't be changed, I preferred to go away. I returned to the West and its necessary ambiguities, which confer to thought its brilliance if not its vigor.

After this, I practiced asceticism in my own way: in my home, in my little world in Paris, where I cut myself off from the city and from life for weeks on end. I lived in a room which was much like a prison cell: large enough for only one. The street noises that reached me were muffled. My horizon became smaller and smaller: I looked only at the Seine bearing along its foam; I no longer perceived the sky mirrored in it. I drew away from people. No tie, no liaison came to interrupt my solitude. I lived only in books, where my memory tried to rejoin a more immense and ordered memory. And the more I remembered, the more I felt excluded and alone.

I felt particularly like a stranger. I had lost my faith, and thus, my sense of belonging and orientation. My faith in life was covered with ashes; my faith in humanity was laughable, childish, sterile; my faith in God was shaken. Things and words had lost their meaning, their axis. An image of the Kabbala described the state of my soul at that time: all of creation had moved from its center in order to exile itself. Whom was I to lean on? What was I to cling to? I was looking for myself, I was fleeing from myself, and always there was this taste of failure, this feeling of defeat inside me.

A member of the Sonderkommando of Treblinka asked himself if one day he would laugh again; another, of Birkenau, wondered if one day he would cry again.

I didn't laugh, I didn't cry. I was silent, and I knew that never would I know how to translate the silence that I carried within myself: again I found myself in the ghetto.

In a sense I am still there. It's natural. I can do nothing about it: the ghetto is in me, in us. It will never leave us. We are its prisoners.

Making the Ghosts Speak

And yet, there has been a change in our behavior. First of all, we express ourselves. I force myself to share the secret that consumes me. I try to make the ghosts within me speak. Does that mean that the wound has healed over? It still burns. I still cannot speak of it. But I can *speak*— that's the change.

A need for communication? For community perhaps? I evoke memories that precede my own; I sing the song of ancient kingdoms; I describe swallowed-up worlds: I exist by what I say as much as by what I keep silent. To protect my silent universe, I speak of the world of others. To avoid painful subjects, I explore others: biblical, Talmudic, Hasidic or contemporary. I evoke Abraham and Isaac so as not to uncover the mystery of my relations with my father. I recount the adventures of the Besht so as not to dwell on the end of his descendants. In other words, literature has become for me a way of making you look away. The tales that I recount are never those that I would like to, or ought to, tell.

The problem is that the essential will never be said or understood. Perhaps I should express my thought more clearly: it's not because I don't speak that you won't understand me; it's because you won't understand me that I don't speak.

That's the problem, and we can do nothing about it: what certain people have lived, you will never live—happily for you, moreover. Their experience has set them apart: they are neither better nor worse, but different, more vulnerable and at the same time more hardened than you. The slightest arrow wounds them, but death does not frighten them. You look at them askance, and they suffer from your look; and yet, they know how to bear the hardest blows, the most bitter disappointments.

This is true for both their relations with the rest of humanity and their relation with God. From God they are awaiting everything, and yet they are aware that everything will scarcely suffice. God himself cannnot change the past; even he cannot negate the fact that the killer has killed 6 million times. How could he redeem himself? I don't know. I suppose that he cannot. Those who claim that this or that constitutes a response to the Holocaust are content with very little.

Things Have Changed

This is what I thought after the war; this is what I still think. And yet, I am surprised to feel a forgotten need to recite certain prayers, to sing certain melodies, to plunge into a certain atmosphere that filled my adolescence. Like everyone, I would give everything I own to awaken and see that we are in 1938–39: that I had only dreamed the future.

I would give much to be able to relive a Sabbath in my small town, somewhere in the Carpathian Mountains. The whiteness of the tablecloths, the blinking candle flames, the beaming faces around me, the melodious voice of my grandfather, the *Hasid* of Vizhnitz, inviting the angels of the Sabbath to accompany him to our home: it pains me even to think of these things.

That is what I miss most: a certain peace, a certain melancholy that the Sabbath, at Sighet, offered its children, big and small, young or old, rich and poor. It is this Sabbath that I miss. Its absence recalls to me all else that is gone. It reminds me that things have changed in the world, that the world itself has changed.

And I have too.

NATHAN A. SCOTT, JR.

Day by Day

The *Century's* question—how has your mind changed over the past ten years?—as I soon came to realize once I began reflecting upon it, is fearfully intimidating, and even bullying. For, as one immediately says to oneself, to take a public platform for the sake of talking about "my mind" and its various shifts and divagations over the past decade must surely be to risk seeming to represent the self-absorption of one who deems himself to be some sort of World-Historical Figure. And, as one thinks of the various testimonies that have come over the years in this series from one's colleagues in the theological community, this uneasiness is not much allayed by what would appear for many of them to have been their unembarrassment over this matter. But then one anxiously says to oneself that to dodge the bid to make some declaration in this vein may suggest lack of engagement with contemporary ferment, may suggest that readiness to talk about how one's mind has changed is prompted merely by some torpor of mind—and the prospect of such a judgment being rendered is, of course, wounding to one's *amour propre*. Yet, even after putting aside all the difficulties and improprieties of this sort that seem to loom, when one does at last face into the question itself, one's ruminations appear dishearteningly not to add up to very much.

"Salad and Dessert"

Here, I suspect, one founders by reason of the manner in which the editors form their question each decennium, for to have it proposed that the bent and atmosphere of one's mind may have *changed* in a relatively brief period of time is to be brought up short before the notion that the life of one's own mind is a kind of drama, an affair of metabases and peripeties and denouements. And so it may be, though we tend, I suspect, most of us, to experience our own inwardness rather more as a fairly steady, though sometimes fitful and devious, engagement with the various particular jobs that the years happen to bring to hand. At least this is how things appear from my own perspective—which is why I must report on the past decade by way merely of a few notations on the sorts of jobs that have come my way.

My field of work, of course, has centered on how the modern literary imagination has dramatized and borne witness to what is problematic in the religious experience of the age. An old friend, James Hastings Nichols (now of Princeton Seminary), when we were colleagues together in the divinity faculty of the University of Chicago in the '50s, once remarked jokingly that mine was a field that formed the salad and dessert of the curriculum, whereas the meat and potatoes were formed by theology and church history, biblical studies and social ethics. Which, though said in a spirit of mischievous good humor, no doubt tellingly registered something of the apathy with which Protestant mentality tends still to regard the world of literature and the arts—for not here, it is felt, does one encounter a locus of the "real."

Contemporary theology consents to relate itself to the philosophical currents of the time (even if only with what is often a halfhearted listlessness) and to social-political dynamics (though by no means managing the prophetic power that was at work in the period of Reinhold Niebuhr). But those movements of the spirit that are astir and manifest in the arts, most especially in the arts of the word, are somehow thought to belong merely to the realm of the oneiric and the fanciful. Which might indeed be the case if literary art specialized, as it is sometimes declared to do, in the purely hypothetical. It does, of course, no doubt represent one great mode of the "possibilizing" power of the imagination—but, when we are dealing, say, with *Heart of Darkness* or the *Duino Elegies* or *Notes Toward a Supreme Fiction* or *Pale Fire*, what is surely to the point is the degree to which certain hypothetical possibilities of human action and experience are so marvelously dramatized by the agencies of *poiesis* that we not only see possibility by way of being transformed into potentiality but see something like a kind of ingression of potentiality into the realm of the actual. And, as my old comrade Amos Wilder is often reminding us, it is just the sort of complicated rendering that the poetic arts are able to give in these terms of "the ordinary universe" that enables them to testify so powerfully to the way we live now, not only in the public sector but, even more, in the deep interiors of the soul. So I have thought it not a bad thing to do to try to plot something of how the cross-questioning may proceed in our period between the religious imagination and the literary imagination.

In the preface I prepared for a 1958 book (*Modern Literature and the Religious Frontier*, Harper & Row) I recorded "my conviction that . . . the literary intelligence is by far the best intelligence of our time, better than the philosophic intelligence, better than the social-scientific . . . and better perhaps even, on the whole, than the theological." And in this and others of my early books (*Rehearsals of Discomposure*, Columbia University Press, 1952; *Albert Camus*, Bowes & Bowes, 1962; *Samuel Beckett*, Bowes and Bowes, 1965; *The Broken Center*, Yale University Press, 1966; *Craters of the Spirit: Studies in the Modern Novel*, Corpus Books, 1968), as I dealt with a variety of modern writers—Dostoevsky, Hardy, Kafka, Lawrence, Eliot, Hemingway, Beckett—I was eager to suggest something like the assertion made by that famous aphorism in William Blake's *The Marriage of Heaven and Hell* which says: "The tygers of wrath are wiser than the horses of instruction." Or, if they have not been wiser, I wanted at least to urge (as I said in that 1958 preface) that they "seem to have traveled farther than most of . . . us and seem to have thrust us more exactly upon the centers of our distress than any other class of [modern intelligentsia] . . . has succeeded in doing." And thus the conviction that most deeply animated my work was that Christian theology, as a result of its dialogue with the great literature of the modern period, will find itself more richly repaid (in terms of deepened awareness both of itself and of the age) than by any other similar transaction it may undertake.

Modernism and Post-Modernism

By the end of the '60s, however, I was turning increasingly from the classic canon of modern literature to those new insurgencies which were lining themselves up behind what specialists in *Tendenz* were beginning to speak of as "post-modernism." And in a 1969 book, *Negative Capability: Studies in the New Literature and the Religious Situation* (Yale University Press), I made my first attempt at reckoning with this range of things. I argued that the chief distinguishing feature of the great avatars of traditionalist modernism—of such figures as Yeats and Pound and Joyce and Mann and Brecht—had been their "rage for order," their search for myths and metaphysics whereby experience might be newly ordered in a period marked by the recession of older codes and beliefs. Whereas those who had followed "the middle generation" of Faulkner and Malraux and Silone and Moravia—such writers as the *nouveau roman* circle of Alain Robbe-Grillet in France, or such Americans as John Barth and Thomas Pynchon and John Hawkes—appeared, as I suggested, to have as their primary quality a Negative Capability, a willingness (as Keats defined it) to subsist "in uncertainties, mysteries, doubts, without any irritable reaching after fact and reason." And it is just in their disinclination to try to subdue or resolve what is recalcitrantly indeterminate and ambiguous in the human scene of our time, in their hesitancy about reaching after any great counterpoise to chaos—it is just in this, I argued, that their difference from classic 20th century modernism mainly consists. I suggested even that this post-modernist temper is expressed in some measure in those contemporary theological styles that are marked by a willingness to make do with "fragments, partial vision, broken speech, not because of the unbelieving world 'out there,' but," as many younger theologians seemed then to be saying, "precisely because that unbelieving world has come to rest within ourselves."[1]

And, with its wariness about the old *profondeurs* and its reticencies about committing itself to large affirmations, I was inclined to regard this whole tendency, in both its literary and its theological aspect, as marked by a kind of authenticity of response to the period that deserved if not endorsement at least a very lenient estimate. But, now, a little more than a decade later, post-modernist literary enterprise increasingly entails a mode of art (especially in the novel) that wants to be merely "self-reflexive," that wants to subvert any expectation of its making reference to a reality extrinsic to its own internal grammar of myth and metaphor; and in seeking, therefore, to offer nothing more than oblique commentary on its own *problématique*, it seems—as one reads the fictions, say, of Thomas Pynchon and Donald Barthelme and Robert Coover and Rudolph Wurlitzer—to represent such a retreat from the public world of our time as does most assuredly make it something very different indeed from the great classic literature of this century.[2] Moreover, that "secular theology" which was at the fore when I was writing *Negative Capability*, though it had the altogether salutary effect of inducing a more stringent kind of honesty among contemporary theologians about what it really means to "make a case," has not itself proved capable of any kind of

---

[1] William Hamilton, *The New Essence of Christianity* (Association, 1961), p. 28.

[2] Such immensely gifted writers as Bellow and Styron and Updike and Percy are, of course, quite outside the ambience being spoken of here, and in them and various others, modernism survives still as a great force, though it may not now carry what Matthew Arnold called "the tone of the centre."

genuinely seminal redintegration. So the whole post-modernist insurgency, as I now feel, requires to be bargained with rather more closely than I was inclined to acknowledge a decade ago.

By the end of the '60s one knew that one had lived through one of the most trying decades of recent American history, more difficult even perhaps in many ways than the crisis years of the 1940s. Indeed, apart from the Black Freedom Movement of the early '60s which had been profoundly enheartening, I was conscious of harboring a good deal of ambivalence about virtually everything the period of Janis Joplin and Tom Hayden and Bishop James Pike and Stokely Carmichael had brought forth. And that ambivalence found expression in two books of the early '70s—*The Wild Prayer of Longing: Poetry and the Sacred* (Yale University Press, 1971) and *Three American Moralists* (University of Notre Dame Press, 1973).

On the one hand, I felt that all the fascinations in that turbulent time with psychedelic ecstasy and polymorphous sexuality, with folk-rock festivals and millenarian communalism, with syncretistic mysticism and "antipolitics"—that all this betokened a nostalgic aspiration for something like what Mircea Eliade has taught us to speak of as "hierophany." To be sure, the people of our age do not ordinarily now take the world to be a *figura* of anything other than or transcendent to itself, and in the first chapter of *The Wild Prayer of Longing* I tried to offer some indication of how the developing history of modern literature reflects the gradual decline and disintegration of the figural perspective. But, once the world is "defiguralized," must it then become something stale and emptied of any kind of high significance? In a remarkable book of the 1950s, *The Inward Morning*, the American philosopher Henry Bugbee at a certain point was raising the question as to "whether we can [still] rejoice with things, or whether [they are] simply inane." And it was a similar question that had been raised by the strange passions that were epidemic in the '60s. Beneath all their flamboyance and antinomianism, the new gypsies and hoboes and hippies and "come-outers" were desperately seeking assurances, as one felt, that "the vulgate of experience" touches a holiness not "beyond reality" but *in* (as Wallace Stevens puts it)

> *The actual landscape with its actual horns*
> *Of baker and butcher blowing . . .*

So in the second chapter of *The Wild Prayer of Longing* I tried to suggest, by recourse to certain ideas of Heidegger, how a sacramental vision of the world may indeed define itself without resort to supernaturalist figuralism. And in the concluding chapter I offered the poetry of Theodore Roethke as a major example in recent literature of "sacramentation" unencumbered by figuralist illusion.

Countering Apocalypticism

But, then, for all of what I found appealing in the religious passions of the period, the "mystical militancy" (as Michael Harrington phrased it) of the New Left—in its terrorist assaults on our universities, in the furiousness of its "confrontation politics," in its grim intention to subvert the civilities of liberal democracy, in its strident demands for Paradise Now—struck me as grievously infected with the disease of apocalypticism. Apocalyptists, in their fastidious distaste for the imperfect realities of this world, find the "radically demanding historical hour"[3] to be intolerable: they want to break things up: they look toward the time when time shall be no more—and their resistance to history, their eagerness to get outside of it altogether, makes for a terribly expensive kind of insobriety, as the events of the '60s amply disclosed. So in *Three American Moralists* I undertook to hold up three enormously gifted writers—Norman Mailer, Saul Bellow and Lionel Trilling—who, as I wanted to suggest, represented a salutary kind of skepticism about what Trilling disdainfully spoke of as "the demand for life as pure spirit." So great, of course, are the differences in style between these three that they might not at first have been thought to form any sort of triad opposed to the rampant apocalypticism of the period: Bellow, as I remarked, is often "the gay lampoonist"—whereas Mailer is "the voluble and adroit *enragé* specializing in the *vita activa*"—and Trilling's style tended to be that of "the learned patrician looking out upon the 'darkling plain,/Swept with confused alarms of struggle and flight.' " But each renders a very severe judgment on those who choose (in a phrase of Bellow's Moses Herzog) to "live a disappointed life," and each presents a testimony that seeks to admonish and embolden us toward recommitting ourselves to the common tasks of the human City, the tasks of building viable forms of *coex*istence. So, amidst the *Kulturkampf* that lay so heavily on the American scene of the '60s and the early '70s, their refusal of any kind of convulsive embrace of Apocalypse gave them, as I argued, the status of public moralists and made them exemplary figures.

In his book of several years ago, *The Feast of Fools*, Harvey Cox assigned

---

[3] Martin Buber, *Pointing the Way* (Harper & Bros., 1957), p. 203.

my writing and that of my Jesuit friends Walter Ong and William Lynch to the genre of "theology of culture," and he expressed some regret that this range of literature "rarely makes any connection" between culture and social-political realities. In regard to my own work, I was somewhat startled by this judgment, and it strikes me as particularly inapposite to *Three American Moralists* and to *The Poetry of Civic Virtue* (Fortress, 1976), whose argument, again, is built around an exemplary triptych—of Eliot, Malraux and Auden. True, I do not in these books treat the literature at hand merely as so much social evidence, but a main part of my intention is to try to illumine significant responses of the literary imagination to some of the larger social and political pressures of the age, and to do so in such a way as to focalize certain of the fundamental religious dilemmas and possibilities that we now face.

Since *The Poetry of Civic Virtue*, apart from the revised and expanded version of an earlier book on Existentialism that Collins issued in 1978 (*Mirrors of Man in Existentialism*) and the long chapter on "Black Literature" I contributed to *The Harvard Guide to Contemporary American Writing* (edited by Daniel Hoffman [Harvard University Press, 1979]), my main literary work has focused on a series of figures (Matthew Arnold, Walter Pater, George Santayana, Wallace Stevens, Martin Heidegger) who make significant proposals regarding the role played by the poetic imagination in the formation of fundamental belief: some of the results of this effort have appeared in the form of essays in journals, and in due course I expect a book to eventuate.

"Making It" Day by Day

But, given now these various labors, do things seem at all different today as compared with a decade ago? Certainly I keep the same basic vocational commitment that has claimed me over the years, and thus nothing at all has altered in this regard. Yet the *deaths* of the past decade—of Reinhold Niebuhr, Wystan Auden, Lionel Trilling, Allen Tate and so many others—have left me with a sense (no doubt inevitable for one of my generation) of terrible deprivation. For most of the people who offered me in my youth the great enabling examples of one or another kind of effort I found myself drawn to are now gone, and thus "making it" day by day now requires a measure of enterprise, of resolution, that one wasn't conscious of having to summon a decade ago.

But this is not the sole difficulty. For when I began my academic career toward the end of the '40s after completing doctoral studies at Columbia,

I had behind me what, as I now realize, I most needed in order even to begin my particular sort of work: namely, a wonderfully vigorous theological enterprise, as well as an enterprise (on the Anglo-American scene) of literary criticism—and I speak carefully—unexampled with respect to the precedent tradition in the splendor of its acuteness and subtlety. In the former connection one need allude only to Barth and Niebuhr and Tillich and Bultmann and Berdyaev to prompt the recollection of numerous others, and in the latter connection the names of Leavis and Empson and Brooks and Winters and Tate will be similarly evocative. The central theological movements of the time, as they aimed at full repossession of the Christian tradition, were untouched by any doubt about the dignity of theology as a field of intelligence or about its capacity to illumine the cultural life of the age. And the vanguard in literary studies conceived it to be the function of the literary imagination to offer the fullest disclosures of what we are seeking to become and of what we must become, and this vanguard took criticism to be the discipline that most centrally focalizes those values that in earlier periods had been furnished by the family or the state, by church or synagogue. Both movements, in other words, were proud and assertive, and one who chose a mediating role in relation to them felt confirmed in this by the remarkable vitalities that were at work.

Already, of course, a decade ago it had become apparent that the terms of the situation were considerably altered, for a great failure of nerve within the theological community had by then begun to be a conspicuous fact of the current scene, enough so indeed for one engaged in my sort of transaction to feel newly disadvantaged. But it was possible then to keep a sense of being still upborne by a critical movement whose faith in the dignity of the literary universe remained intact. And I now marvel at how rapidly over the past decade that faith, too, has become a casualty of the times. For, over these past ten years, as the strange doctrines of structuralist ideology have drifted across the Atlantic from Paris into the forums of American criticism, the gifted young and many of the gifted middle-aged have learned (under the tutelage of such people as Jacques Derrida and Michel Foucault and the late Roland Barthes) to specialize in one or another mode of what is called "deconstruction." The new orthodoxy lays it down that the language of literary texts only doubles back on itself, and thence on to the language of other texts to which it is related by the logic of *intertextualité*, and thence on to that general *system* of signification (*langue*) of which the given text is merely an epiphenomenon. So, however much the "poem" may seem to promise mediation of the "world," this pledge needs at last to be adjudged something spurious, mired as the poem is in a universe of absolute linguisticality. In short, the figurative impulse leads nowhere beyond sheer figuration itself, and literary art is therefore quite "blind" with respect to the world "out there"; it has no "meaning": it exhibits only a play of tropes whose mercuriality "forbids . . . [the text] to be read as an 'organic unity' organized around some version of the *logos.*"[4] And thus the task of criticism is to "deconstruct" or nullify what may *appear* to be those intimations given off by the poem of a coherent account of human experience. It is such notions as these that now make up the "folk mythology" of the more advanced clerks of literary criticism and theory.

Which is to say that, in regard to my own kind of work, I find the weathers of contemporary intellectual life to be rather more incongenial today than I felt them to be a decade ago. And in this darkening time I also find myself touched ever more keenly by the pathos in those words uttered at the end of his life by the writer Dencombe in Henry James's story "The Middle Years": "We work in the dark—we do what we can—we give what we have. Our doubt is our passion, and our passion is our task."

---

[4] J. Hillis Miller, "On Edge: The Crossways of Contemporary Criticism," *Bulletin of the American Academy of Arts and Sciences*, Vol. XXXII, No. 4 (January 1979), p. 19.

FREDERICK BUECHNER

All's Lost, All's Found

"How my mind has changed in the last decade" is the subject to which I've been invited to address myself, and since the invitation seemed to offer a certain amount of leeway, I've undertaken to produce less a formal essay than a few rather informal paragraphs under three different headings. To begin with, *How my mind has changed about myself.*

Like a Child

My readings in Buddhism have long since convinced me that when I talk about myself, I don't really know what I'm talking about. "How do I learn to control myself? To understand myself? To live with myself?" the harried occidental goes to the Buddhist monk to inquire, and after 20 minutes or so of properly inscrutable silence, the monk says something like, "Show me this self you're fretting about. Then maybe I can help you with it." Needless to say, the point seems to be that when you come right down to it, there's nothing to show. I do not have a self. I *am* a self. As soon as I draw back to scrutinize "it," I have by the very act of drawing back removed from my scrutiny the very thing I seek to know. So instead of trying to talk about who I am, let me simply describe something of what it feels like to live inside my skin now, let's say, instead of in 1970.

In many ways it feels much the same. In my 50s as in my 40s, I feel much of the time like a child. I get excited about the kinds of things that excite a ten-year-old. The first snow of the year, for instance. The sound of rain on the roof. Buying things, especially books, which are less important for me to read than simply to have. Getting things in the mail. Going to the movies. Having somebody remember my name. Remembering somebody's name. Making a decent forehand in tennis. Being praised. Chocolate ice cream. And so on.

Like a child too, I feel uneasy in the presence of people who are more grown-up than I am. I find myself saying to them less what I really feel like saying than what I feel they'd like to have me say. When people are taking me seriously as a grown-up—listening to me lecture or preach or talking to me about one of my books—I think to myself, *if they only knew.* If someone were to wake me up in the middle of the night with a flashlight in my eyes and, before I had time to think, were to ask me who I was, I would say not my grown-up name but my child name. If I were asked my age, I would say not 53 but 23. Maybe even 13. Given the choice of having flying saucers, the Loch Ness monster, ghosts, magic and miracles generally proven either true or false, I would choose them to be true without a moment's hesitation. And so on again.

The child in me is very much alive, in other words, and though this involves certain serious disadvantages, I would not have it otherwise. A child is apt to see certain things better than his elders, I think, because, less sure than they of what to *expect*, he is more apt than they to see what, actually though unexpectedly, *is.* By the same token, a child is apt to feel certain things more than his elders too because he is not as good as they at keeping his feelings under control, and even though this makes him vulnerable to some emotional inanities that maturity is relatively safe from, I still would not have it any other way.

All of this was as true of me in 1970 as now, but there have been changes too. One instance of this is the word that I find I've started to use for sighing with. Instead of the traditional *oh dear* or *oh well* or any of those, again and again I hear myself saying *child, child* in a tone of voice that seems to be a sort of weary reproof and yet a kind of lament too. *Don't be so foolish,* the grown-up in me says to the child. Don't make such a fuss. Don't let the world get under your skin so. Keep your guard up more. Stay on an evener keel. Grow up. That is the reproof.

The lament, I think, stems from knowing that the reproof will be heeded all too well. Already the child *is* keeping his guard up more, keeping the world at arm's length more, starting to see less, feel less. It is a step toward maturity and, as such, to be rejoiced in. But it is a step away from something in its way equally precious and, as such, to be lamented in, too. *Child, child* . . . I feel a state of being, a dimension of selfhood, coming to an end, and it is proper that it should, so that something richer and wiser and, in the long run, even holier can take its place. But the end of anything is sad because the end of anything foreshadows the end, finally, of everything. And that final end is death, about which also my mind has changed, and hence the second heading: *How my mind has changed about death.*

Death as Nonevent

Even 40 years ago, let alone ten, I knew that like everybody else I would die someday, and in my mind I had already died several times. I have never had an ache or pain that wasn't fatal or an illness that wasn't terminal. One of the occupational hazards of being a writer of fiction is to have an imagination as overdeveloped as a blacksmith's right arm. Again and again I have watched the doctor pause for a way to break the tragic news to me. I have lain in a hospital room receiving the final visits of friends. I have said good-bye to my wife and children for the last time. I have attended my own funeral.

There is something to be said for such nonsense. For one thing, to have the doctor tell you that it is not lung cancer after all but just a touch of the flu is, in a way, to be born again. For another thing, it is to be given back not just your old life again but your old life with a new sense of its pricelessness. For a time at least, old grievances, disappointments, irritations, failures that had cast a shadow over your days suddenly cease to matter much. You are alive. That's all that matters, and the sheer wonder and grace of it are staggering, the sense of life as a gift, and the sense of the pricelessness of each moment too, even the most humdrum. The smell of breakfast. The trip to pick up the laundry. The walk with a friend. They were nearly taken away for good. Someday they will be taken away for good indeed. But in the meantime they are yours. Treasure them for what they are. Treasure them for what they will not be forever. Treasure them for what, except by God's grace, they might never have been at all.

All of this was part of what it was like to be me in 1970 and continues to be so now, but at some point during the intervening decade I experienced death in a new way still. I tried to describe the experience in a novel called *Open Heart*. There is a scene in which a man goes to visit his sister Miriam's grave in a Brooklyn cemetery. He tries to shed a tear for her, but the tear won't come. Instead, his mind begins to wander until in a sense it wanders off altogether, and he ends up just staring down at the grass so hard that he doesn't even see it. He doesn't have a thought in his head. What follows next he describes like this:

> I was still standing there in this kind of empty-headed trance, and then it was like what happens when, just as you're about to go to sleep at night, you seem to trip over something and can feel the whole bed shake under you. I *came to,* I suppose you would say. Some stirring in the air or quick movement of squirrel or bird brought me back to myself, and just at that instant of being brought back to myself, I

knew that the self I'd been brought back to was some fine day going to be as dead as Miriam. I knew it not just in the usual sense of knowing it but knew it in almost the Biblical sense of having sex with it. I knew I didn't just *have* a body. I *was* a body. It was like walking into a closet door at night. The thud of it jolted me down to the roots of my hair.

The body I was was going to be dead. I'd known it before, but here I banged right into it—not a lesson this time but a collision. You might say that there at my sister's grave I finally lost my innocence, saw the unveiling of middle-ages's last and most intimate secret. There in Brooklyn I was screwed by my own death.

At some point during the past ten years, in other words, I came, like the narrator in the novel, to know my death in a new way. What I had feared as a hypochondriac came to seem, by comparison, a small thing or, more accurately, a constellation of small things. I had feared the pain and indignity of disease. I had feared hospitals—the smell, the sterility, the depersonalization. I had dreaded the last farewells. I had dreaded leaving the party while I was still having a good time. I had feared and dreaded the ultimate separation from everything and everybody I held most dear. But behind all these fears, and essential to their fearsomeness, was the presupposition that the self that I am would be in some sense around to experience them, down to and including my own funeral.

What I have come to experience since, and with a degree of immediacy impossible to describe, is the extinction of the self itself. With something more than my imagination I have come at odd moments to experience something more than my death—that is to say, something more than my death as an event in which my self will participate. I have come to experience it as a nonevent in which I will no longer have or be a self to participate with. Call it Nothingness. Call it the End. And the curious thing is that when it comes to this most staggering reality of all, I am no longer afraid.

Dying and dissolution continue to strike fear in me. Death itself does not. Ten years ago if somebody had offered me a vigorous, healthy life that would never end, I would have said Yes. Today I think I would say No. I love my life as much as I ever did and will cling on to it for as long as I can, but life without death has become as unthinkable to me as day without night or waking without sleep. Which brings me to the third and final heading, which is *How my mind has changed about God.*

Letting Go

Needless to say, this one is closely related to the other two. The child in me must die so that the man in me can be born. Yet the man in me must die too, all of me, the most that I have it in my power to become as well as the least out of whose demise the most emerges. And yet timorous, overimaginative, doom-ridden, life-loving, self-serving and -centered and sinful as I am, I find that I contemplate this fact with a new and curious absence of fear. Why should this be so?

By way of an answer, I find myself drawing again from a novel, this time a new one titled *Godric*. It has to do with a medieval hermit-saint who for many years chastened his flesh in the icy waters of the River Wear near the city of Durham in northern England. As a very old man he describes the experience of bathing in it in the dead of winter:

> First there's the fiery sting of cold that almost stops my breath, the aching torment in my limbs. I think I may go mad, my wits so outraged that they seek to flee from my skull like rats a ship that's going down. I puff. I gasp. Then inch by inch a blessed numbness comes. I have no legs, no arms. My very heart grows still. These floating hands are not my hands. The ancient flesh I wear is rags for all I feel of it.
>
> "Praise, praise!" I croak. Praise God for all that's holy, cold, and dark. Praise him for all we lose, for all the river of the years bears off. Praise him for stillness in the wake of pain. Praise him for emptiness. And as you race to spill into the sea, praise him yourself, old Wear. Praise him for dying and the peace of death.
>
> In the little church I built of wood for Mary, I hollowed out a place for him. Perkin brings him by the pail and pours him in. Now that I can hardly walk, I crawl to meet him there. He takes me in his chilly lap to wash me of my sins. Or I kneel down beside him till within his depths I see a star.
>
> Sometimes this star is still. Sometimes she dances. She is Mary's star. Within that little pool of Wear she winks at me. I wink at her. The secret that we share I cannot tell in full. But this much I will tell. What's lost is nothing to what's found, and all the death that ever was, set next to life, would scarcely fill a cup.

At the age of 100 the old man knows what at the age of 53 I am only just beginning to see: that if it is by grace we are saved, it is by grace too that we are lost—or lost, at least, in the sense of losing our selves, our lives, our all. In the past, when my faith was strong, I always trusted God more or less. I trusted him with my life, which is to say I trusted him, but with the presupposition that I would always be in some measure alive to say to him, in the words of the *Te Deum*, "Oh Lord, in thee have I trusted;

let me never be confounded," meaning that I would always be around to cajole with him, plead with him, and in general to remind him to be the God of mercy and love I always trusted him to be. The change is that now I begin, at least, to trust him with my death. I begin, at least, to see that death is not merely a biological necessity but a necessity too in terms of the mystery of salvation.

We find by losing. We hold fast by letting go. We become something new by ceasing to be something old. This seems to be close to the heart of that mystery. I know no more now than I ever did about the far side of death as the last letting-go of all, but I begin to know that I do not need to know and that I do not need to be afraid of not knowing. God knows. That is all that matters.

Out of Nothing he creates Something. Out of the End he creates the Beginning. Out of selfness we grow, by his grace, toward selflessness, and out of that final selflessness, which is the loss of self altogether, "Eye hath not seen, nor ear heard, neither have entered into the heart of man" what new marvels he will bring to pass next. All's lost. All's found. And if such words sound childish, so be it. Out of each old self that dies some precious essence is preserved for the new self that is born, and within the child-self that is part of us all, there is perhaps nothing more precious than the fathomless capacity to trust.

IV

The Global Setting: Liberation as an Enduring Theme

HARVEY COX

Theology: What Is It?
Who Does It? How Is It Done?

> I wondered then [1966] why theologians can be so aware of the insti-
> tutional and historical setting of *other* people's theology and so uncriti-
> cal about their own. I thought that what we really needed to learn
> from the Marxists ... [was] how the theologian's *locus* in the class
> structure and power fabric of his society influences his theology. The
> trouble is that I still think that's true, and that when your readers see
> that they'll think my mind has not changed. And everybody knows a
> theologian's mind *must* change every ten years. Otherwise, why the
> series?

The citation above is taken from my contribution to the 1970 version of
this series, in which I recalled what I had written for an interim series in
1966. In rereading both of these previous articles, I was surprised at the
constancy, maybe even doggedness, of my theological preoccupations.
Perhaps that is only to be expected. Still, my invitation to contribute to
the 1980–81 series has for some reason made me vaguely suspicious, not
just of my own previous forays but also of the series itself and what it has
meant for theology.

That Sniff of Suspicion
I could, of course, simply repress my uneasiness and just barge ahead
and write. It wouldn't be the first time. Still, "the hermeneutics of suspicion" suggests another course: not to bury my queasiness but to explore
its significance. Truly critical theology always begins with that sniff of
suspicion. One feels disquieted about the *way* a question is asked, the
unspoken assumptions of any intellectual enterprise.
Maybe this series is an example of something about which we ought to
be at least a little suspicious. It is, after all, an integral part of the history
it records. The editors, by deciding who will be invited to write (and who

will not be invited), delineate the limits of the permissible. The contributors in turn, taking their signals from the history of the series as well as from the kind of writing that has produced the invitation, will then demonstrate *what* theology is and *how* it is produced. Little of this will happen through explicit argument. But since implicit messages are usually more important than manifest ones (they communicate "deep structures" rather than transient content), and since they are the part of the message that is least often subjected to critical examination, it seems doubly important to examine them in the case of this series.

Good. Already my sniffing has turned up something worth further pursuit. Although so far it may all sound grippingly commonsensical, please stay with me. The most formative ideas of any age are the ones viewed as commonsensical or self-evident, so the chances are that we have already blundered into the hiding place of three of the most influential assumptions present in the world of theology today: namely, *what* theology is, *how* it is done and *who* does it. It is about these questions that my mind may be changing. Let us see.

A Theology of the Elite

Who then does theology? By now it has become tiresome to keep pointing out that "theologians," including the ones who have made this series so influential, have been preponderantly white, male, Euro-American, etc. Indeed, the *Century*'s present editors, as aware as anyone of this criticism, will undoubtedly include red, black, brown, female and non-Euro-American figures on this year's invitation list. It will be much harder, however, to avoid the characterization made a few years back by Philip Scharper that "most of the theologians—Protestant and Catholic—who have had such a heavy influence on American theologians and American theology have tended to be, almost by definition, members of the upper-middle class, indeed forming something of an intellectual elite" (*Catholic Mind*, April 1976, p. 18). This is a problem that even the most skillful editorial selection cannot avoid. Why?

The reason this *class* bias is so stubborn is clear. The minimal conditions (could we even call them "means of production"?) for doing theology, even for writing such an article as this, include the ability to read and write in at least one language, some familiarity with the received tradition of concepts and categories, sufficient leisure to think, and the power to get one's ideas published or otherwise heard. But these conditions are available only to people who have benefited from privileged educational opportunities and whose present position in life frees them from a daily struggle against hunger and cold. These minimal "class" conditions exclude the vast majority of people from ever being considered theologians, at least in this respect.

I am not interested in scolding. Theology has always been produced by an elite, and although the voices of blacks, feminists and other previously excluded groups have undercut some established perspectives, they have not done much to challenge the class bias. What I am asking is whether the conditions that automatically exclude all but middle-class people from doing theology make a significant difference *in the theology itself*, including my theology. Or is it something one can safely ignore? This consideration moves us on to the question of *how* theology is done.

A New Blade

In the past two centuries Christian theologians have become increasingly self-critical about how theology is done, especially about sources and procedures. This capacity for self-criticism has often been regarded as the most important single theological development of that period. The question I keep asking myself now, however, is whether theologians are prepared to take the next step, that of moving from a historical-critical to a sociocritical method. This step would move us beyond the sharp awareness we now have, for example, of how the rhetorical conventions and cultural symbols of any period shape even its most original theology, to a recognition of how the pervasive ideology of the dominant class in any society influences the theology it produces. As the Jesuit theologian Alfred T. Hennelly says, we now need a new "Ockham's razor" to be used for "the careful dissection of the manifold relationships that exist between the ideology of the western ruling elites and the development of western theology."

A new Ockham's razor? Yes, I think we need one. The first one, it will be recalled, was invented by the 14th century Franciscan theologian William of Ockham to pare away the superfluous from the essential. Ockham believed that an "overloaded" concept inevitably suffered distortion. Likewise, because of the class position of those who write it, most theology today is freighted with an overload of the dominant class ideology. The trouble is that while most theologians are trained to watch out for historical biases and logical non sequiturs, we are rarely taught how to recognize the distortion a dominant ideological perspective imposes on our own or other people's theological work. *The Christian Cen-*

tury's series, by example and not by intent, continues by and large to hold up this truncated model of a less-than-critical theology which proceeds without much awareness of its own class bias.

Since this dominant model of *how* theology should be done is perpetuated by implicit example, a counterproposal needs to be made explicit. My thesis here is that no theology that claims to be "critical" can continue to ignore this ideological-critical dimension. Understanding how the dominant ideology of any society, including our own, becomes a latent but potent element in the production of theology should be an integral, not just an ancillary, part of the theological enterprise itself. Ockham's razor needs a new blade. This moves us on to the next question to which the *Century's* series supplies an implicit answer: the question of *what* theology is.

In the Western intellectual tradition, a serious hiatus has developed over the past few centuries between the study of religious and theological ideas *as such*, including their internal relations to each other, on the one hand, and the study of the historical and political *significance* of theological formulations in human societies on the other. The first task is usually thought of as "theology," while the second—with its parallel or "dialectical" concern for how social reality influences theological ideas—is generally turned over to other disciplines. Again, by and large, the *Century's* series reproduces this hiatus.

I believe that this separation is a serious mistake. It arose historically along with the modern fragmentation of the disciplines, the overspecialization of intellectual labor, and the separation of church and state. But its danger is that it leads to just that ethereal view of theology which obscures its social sources and thereby disguises its ideological significance. If a strong sociocritical element were built into theology, this separation would not be possible. The integration of this dimension into our theological work, as a part of *what* theology is, constitutes an urgent need. To put it another way, theology must be its own most informed critic. It must constantly expand its awareness not just of its own internal processes but of how it influences and is influenced by its milieu.

Ideology and Ideas

So far I have not gone much beyond what I said in 1970. In that article I also wrote: "*All* thinking, including theological thinking, arises *in part* as ideology; that is, in defense of this or that institution's power and privilege."

The idea is not new. I wonder, then, *why* most theologians have been so hesitant to enter into the next phase, the sociocritical phase, of theological history. Could it be because most of us suspect that it would confront us with some embarrassing contradictions which other fields could more easily avoid? How can members of a privileged elite be the interpreters of a Message which so ringingly challenges all established power and all elites? The question is a serious one, and it requires me to go beyond my 1970 thoughts on the subject.

Despite the obvious difficulties middle-class theologians face in this regard, I do not believe that middle-classness *as such* necessarily prevents anyone from doing Christian theology. The notion that class automatically "determines" ideas is not defended by any serious class analyst today. It is as dead as that equally quaint notion that ideas appear by inspiration or insight and without reference to the impinging social reality. But the ghost of the mechanical-determinist idea still haunts the intellectual world, functioning as a favorite straw man to be pummeled by those who need a horrible example of reductionism to warn us against the dire peril of investigating the relationship among class, ideology and ideas.

The fact is, however, that the relationship between ideology and ideas (and vice versa) *can* be laid open—and with a scalpel (or a razor), not with a meat cleaver. A fecund tradition of Marxist literary criticism—including such figures as Lucien Goldmann, Walter Benjamin and Georg Lukács—can help us see how. But no theologian can even begin to slice through the ideological gristle of a text or to prevent her or his own work from being ideologically "overdetermined" without passing through one indispensable first step: the recognition that such ideological distortion does occur. Only after this initial recognition can one go on to learn *how* it occurs and how to minimize it in one's own case.

The inventor of Muzak once claimed that the great success of his invention lay in the simple fact that one never notices it until it is turned off. The same is true of ideology. What is needed, as Karl Mannheim pointed out years ago in *Ideology and Utopia*, is a knowledge of how to spot and deal with something which by its very nature eludes most forms of detection. Although we can easily discern someone else's ideology if it is different from ours (liberation theologians, for example, are constantly accused of being "too ideological"), we have a desperately difficult time recognizing our own. "Theirs" is patent and obtuse. Our own ideology, however, passes itself off as the obvious or even as "standards of scholarly excellence." But as the literary critics I have just mentioned lucidly demonstrate, the task of recognizing and analyzing ideology is not impossible. It can be done.

Resign from the Middle Class?

The first step is to lay aside any possibility of simply jumping out of one's class skin. Intellectuals gain absolutely nothing by lamenting the fact that they were not born with a different gender or pigmentation or into a different social stratum. Worse, the pious lamentation itself can often become a symbolic substitute for an effective critical method. Class bias is not dissolved by religious ecstasy or heroic imagination. This is why I believe that the well-intentioned phrase "identifying with the poor" is misleading in two ways.

First, "identification" is too psychologistic and can easily pass over into a neo-Franciscan romanticism. Whatever the values of voluntary poverty, the most salient characteristic of real poverty is that it is *not* voluntary. Poverty is not just penury. It is also powerlessness. Education, social skills, "contacts" and experience in the dominant culture are all part of what it means to be "nonpoor," and since none of these can simply be shed, even someone who has embraced voluntary poverty or some kind of simpler life style remains middle class in the most important respects.

Second, as anyone who has lived among the poor for any length of time knows, the dominant ideology has also impressed itself on the consciousness of poor people. They often follow it with a vengeance. Middle-class theologians only deceive themselves if they think they can just resign from the middle class.

Still, class is not fate. Classes come into existence in history and they exist only in conflict with each other. Therefore, "class" is a political and social category, not an ontological one. This means that middle-class theologians (including black and feminist and Third World theologians) *can* learn how to uncover and deal with the dominant ideological component of theology, but the strategy for doing so must be a political-social strategy commensurate with the nature of class itself. How can this be done?

Encountering the "Rival Sibling"

In my view, the problem the theologian faces in this respect is not essentially different from the one faced by any other intellectual who is interested in becoming critically aware of her or his own class perspective. The method for dealing with the problem is similar also. Antonio Gramsci, the Italian Marxist whose writings have undergone such a remarkable renaissance in recent years, especially as we search for a more "Western" and democratic form of socialism, was fascinated with this issue. Gramsci kept asking himself throughout his life how so many intellectuals both in past historical periods and in his own time, people who were not an integral part of the poor or working classes, could nonetheless give essential leadership to people's liberation movements. How did these intellectuals come to understand and neutralize their own bondage to dominant class ideologies?

Gramsci's answer, put very simply, is that the issue of *how* one does intellectual work eventually comes down to the question of *for whom* one does it. For Gramsci, this was a matter not of goodwill but of social location.

Intellectuals, Gramsci suggested, occupy a kind of no-man's land between the principal classes. As mental workers who live off what they write or teach, they sell the product of their own labor. They are not capitalists. But the style and pace of the work they do as artisans (their "work process," a central category in Marxist analysis) is still largely in their own hands, which is not the case for factory workers. For Gramsci, this contradictory position of intellectuals has both advantages and disadvantages. Not totally ensconced in any single class, the intellectual artisan-worker is in a better position to *choose* where her or his loyalties will be invested.

But there is a trap to be avoided. Since in capitalist society the intellectual is not structurally part of the working class, and since nearly all opportunities for intellectual employment are within institutions directed by the ruling classes, the tendency to allow oneself to be molded by the dominant ideology and to become one of its—albeit unconscious—perpetuators is very powerful. How, then, do critical intellectuals become aware of this danger and exercise the choice they have to avoid perpetuating the dominant-pervasive ideology? (Note that I am not dealing here with those intellectuals who consciously decide to champion the dominant ideology.) How does the dominant ideology become visible to someone who might well remain unconsciously under its sway?

The English literary critic Terry Eagleton, who stands in the tradition of Goldmann and Lukács, answers this question eloquently:

> Ideology, seen from within, has no outside; in this sense one does not transgress its outer limits as one crosses a geographical boundary . . . It is impossible to come to its frontiers from within . . . in discovering its demarcations, ideology discovers its self-dissolution; it cannot sur-

vive the "culture shock" consequent on its stumbling into alien territory adjacent to itself. . . . It cannot survive the traumatic recognition
of its own repressed parentage—the truth that it is not after all self-
reproductive but was historically brought to birth. . . . Such a recognition may be forced upon ideology by the unwelcome discovery of a
rival sibling—an antagonistic ideology which reveals to it the secret of
its own birth [*Criticism and Ideology,* pp. 95–96].

Put more prosaically, the only way to become aware of one's own ideology is to see one's work *through the mirror of another ideology.* For theologians working in institutions dominated by the prevailing ideology of
careerism, individualism, scholarly objectivity and the rest, this "encounter with the rival sibling" is essential. It requires us to look at our
work from the perspective of those who are oppressed by that ideology
and who are therefore actively trying to expose it and to transform the
society of which it is a part.

The German theologian F. W. Marquardt suggests that whatever other
value Marxist thought may have, for the theologian who works in a capitalist milieu it provides an indispensable heuristic device with which to
expose her or his unreflective "bourgeois" assumptions. I think Marquardt is right as far as he goes. Today, Marxism is the rival sibling. But
his suggestion still depends on the continuing personal goodwill of the
individual theologian. For Gramsci, on the other hand, the matter was
not one of goodwill but of *accountability.* It is a question not in the first
instance of what one reads (though that is obviously important) but of *for
whom* one works—as distinguished from *by whom* one is remunerated. All
intellectuals need an accountability network since thinking is by its nature a social process. The question for Gramsci was this: Which accountability community will it be?

The "OK" Agenda

Gramsci's formula provides an effective antidote to the way the dominant ideology actually influences intellectual work. As the French critic
Pierre Macherey has observed (*Pour une Théorie de la Production Littéraire*),
ideology shapes a text more in what is not said than in what is said. It
makes itself felt in what is left out, in what the feminist writer Tillie
Olsen calls "the silences."

Ideology also makes its impact at the level of agendas and priorities.
The dominant classes have certain questions they would like to have ad-
dressed and other questions they would prefer not to have aired. The
"OK" questions are the ones around which conferences are organized

and for which research grants and travel fellowships are made available. The approved agenda also influences what counts as "careful," "thoughtful" and, most of all, "responsible" work. Not even the best-intentioned intellectual can avoid this agenda because of the imbalance between the way its pressures are felt (as subtle, reasonable and built into the fabric of institutional relations) and the way those of an alternative agenda are felt (as "outside," diversionary, professionally unproductive).

Accountability does not come naturally. True, in a capitalist society, accountability to the dominant ideology *appears* to be spontaneous, but it appears so because that ideology informs the mechanisms by which accountability is institutionalized. This means that an alternative form of accountability must be a matter of self-conscious selection. It must be self-imposed.

This question of accountability structures is an especially important one for feminists, Third World people, blacks and other minority students who are learning theology at institutions directed by the dominant classes. It is critical for such students to understand that they already have—at least in principle—an alternative accountability structure. The latent but powerful influence of theological education, however, can often move them out of that community and into forms of accountability provided by the dominant culture. If this pressure is not resisted, such students will soon find themselves reproducing dominant ideologies along with everyone else.

For the practicing theologian the task is even more difficult. To place oneself in an alternative accountability structure runs counter to many of the career patterns and associational forms of academic intellectuals. Also, as I have already mentioned, since the dominant ideology permeates not only the middle classes but—through the device Gramsci called "cultural hegemony"—the working and poor classes as well, the intellectual cannot settle for some kind of "identification with the poor." Rather than "identification" I prefer the more political term "alliance." Rather than with "the poor," these alliances should link us to those groups that are actively opposing the dominant society and its ideology. And this can become both personally and professionally risky. Still, it is not impossible. It involves discovering those newly emergent social locations, forums, problems and "standards of scholarship" within which many intellectuals and some theologians are already working. It raises the question of "for whom" one does theology.

In his own way, Karl Barth sensed the priority of the question of "for whom" one does theology—what we have called *accountability*. Barth rejected the idea that one does theology for the guild, or for the profession, or for the academy. He saw that it was crucial for him to declare as unequivocally as possible that he was accountable first of all to the church. He was a "church theologian" and was careful to inscribe this reminder in the title of his major opus. Friedrich Schleiermacher, on the other hand, declared in his most widely read work that he considered those for whom he wrote to be the "cultured despisers of religion."

New Interlocutors

I appreciate the fact that both Barth and Schleiermacher were so explicit about their intended "interlocutors"—that is, the people to whom they listened, for whom they wrote and from whom they wanted a response. In this respect, they both did much better than many present-day theologians who are never quite clear on this, perhaps the most critical methodological issue of all. Still, I think we must move beyond both Barth and Schleiermacher on this question of accountability.

In a passing reference to Jesus' statement that "the Sabbath is made for man, not man for the Sabbath," Juan Luis Segundo puts the question with characteristic bluntness. Does not this statement, he asks, mean today "that human life in society, liberated as far as possible from alienations, constitutes the absolute value, and that all religious institutions, all dogmas, all the sacraments and all ecclesiastical authorities have only a relative, that is, a functional value?"

I think Segundo is right, and this means that we can no longer be merely church theologians in any institutional sense. The coming of the Kingdom of God through the angry poor and the disinherited, both inside and outside the church, must provide our accountability structure. It also means that we cannot address our theology to the questions and concerns of the "cultured despisers" of religion, since to converse mainly with them does nothing to crack open the dominant ideology we share with them or to change the society which that ideology helps perpetuate.

Whenever my ideas have changed over the past ten years, it has been because new conversation partners, new critics, have raised new questions. Maybe what we all need most in theology today is a new Ockham's razor and new interlocutors to help us learn how to use it.

ROSEMARY RADFORD RUETHER

Asking the Existential Questions

Reflecting on one's intellectual development prematurely may be a mistake. A relatively young scholar may easily confuse fragmentary and tentative ventures with significant and formative patterns of thought and action. Nevertheless, as I look back over a journey of approximately 25 years, since I was first catapulted into intense intellectual activity at the beginning of my college work, I can discern certain basic patterns of thought and action that I have followed. These patterns show up as movement in a great variety of directions; sometimes they have been formulated as conscious principles, sometimes manifested more as a gut instinct for what is "right." I will discuss these in terms of four large areas of personal reflection and social action: (1) the relation of Christianity to other religions; (2) the relation of Roman Catholic Christianity to other Christian bodies; (3) the relation of American identity to anti-American criticism; and (4) the relation of feminism to male-dominated culture and institutions.

My intellectual questions and research have never been purely theoretical. I have in every case dealt with existential questions about how I was to situate my life, my identity, my commitments. I have never taken up an intellectual issue which did not have direct connections with clarifying and resolving questions about my personal existence, about how I should align my existence with others, ideologically and socially. This is true of my research into the rise of Christology or the formation of the doctrine of the afterlife in late biblical Judaism as much as it is of my more obviously contemporary, topical writing.

In this sense all my varied intellectual interests have cohered in one way or another as an interaction of reflection and practice. This may actually be true of all intellectual life, although our concepts of "pure research" tend to deny it. But I suspect that it tends to be more consciously and concretely the case with those whose identities do not cohere readily with the dominant systems of thought and society.

Christianity's Credibility

The question of the church's claims of faith and morality vis-à-vis the other traditions of world culture was posed for me early in my academic career. Much of the church's record of social morality appeared discreditable. The problem of the church's moral and intellectual record was aggravated, in the Roman Catholic context, by the hierarchy's inability to admit to serious error in official policy (infallibility means never having to say you're sorry!). That the church as a historical body had made serious errors, such as justifying slavery or sexism, did not surprise me. But the fact that it has been unable to admit error is a serious problem for the church's understanding of its own humanity, as well as of the Christian message of salvation through repentance and forgiveness of sins. The inability of this church to resolve any of the serious pastoral dilemmas that beset it is rooted in this authority problem.

But the credibility of Christianity became suspect for me also in its foundations, not just in its later development. Things did not happen the way the official history said they did. Key ideas, such as Christology and the Trinity, had a hidden pedigree in Near Eastern and Greco-Roman religion and philosophy that contradicted the biblical heritage from which these ideas purportedly were derived. These questions launched me on a wide-ranging search into Christian origins. By unraveling the strands of early Christian development and tracing them to their sources, I hoped to discover what it could mean to me.

During this period (1954–60) I was influenced by two brilliant classicists, Robert Palmer and Philip Merlan at Claremont. Both of these men preferred the culture and philosophy of Greco-Roman antiquity to Christianity. Their perspective transformed my stance toward Christianity. I learned to look at the whole Judeo-Christian tradition through the eyes of those alternative communities in antiquity that were defeated by the church. The triumphalistic presumptions about the superiority of Yahwism to Ba'alism, Christianity to paganism were no longer possible. Both biblical and nonbiblical faiths seemed to me to have good and bad points. If Christianity finally won, it was not because of its absolute difference but rather because of its ability to absorb all the viable elements of ancient Mediterranian cultures into a new synthesis. But the synthesis was itself a peculiar one and posed problems of reappropriation for today.

These questions directed me to research into early Christian development in relation to a number of specific issues. I was particularly concerned with the intersection of intellectual constructs and particular social conflicts. My Ph.D. thesis on *Gregory Nazianzus: Rhetor and Philosopher* (Cambridge University Press, 1969), as well as my research into patristic sexism, anti-Semitism and Christology, reflects these concerns.

A period of estrangement from biblical religion in favor of alternative perspectives eventually led me back to a positive interest in Christianity and then to a clarified identification with it. If Christianity was the only viable synthesis of the traditions and cultures that remained at the end of the ancient world, then it is Christianity itself which represents the most interesting legacy of this era of human consciousness. But I am always aware that I reappropriate Christianity from a markedly different basis than do traditional Christians. I reject absolutist views of biblical religion, while at the same time finding biblical religion in its Christian form the most viable language *for me* to express the dialectics of human existence in relation to God. I believe that God has truly spoken through Christianity. But God is not a "Christian" and does not prefer Christians (or Jews) to the rest of humanity.

As I began to clarify my Christian identity, I asked what form of Christianity would best fit my sensibilities. The Protestant critical consciousness was academically helpful, but Protestant worship life lacked depth for me. I had grown up as a Roman Catholic, but in an ecumenical atmosphere. My father and his family were Anglicans. Other friends and relatives were Jews, Unitarians and Quakers. Along with Catholic worship I also at various times attended Episcopal or Quaker worship. But these others were not "mine" in the same way that the Roman Catholic community was. This I have come to regard as more a matter of ecclesial "ethnicity" than of points of "superiority."

Catholicism and Ecumenism

The unleashing of the waves of renewal through the Second Vatican Council was undoubtedly a crucial fact in my development at this stage. Instead of a church sealed off against self-doubt, there suddenly appeared a church engaged in intense self-questioning. This development made Catholicism an exciting and open community within which to contribute my insights. The 1960s occurred for me between the ages of 23 and 32. This means that a critical state of my adult identity coalesced both with the decade of Catholic renewal and the decade of American social crisis. If I had been born ten years earlier, I might well stand in a different place today.

The renewal of Catholicism meant that a whole host of teachings became open questions for at least a significant sector of Catholic Christians. These ranged from current pastoral conflicts over birth control to the basic questions of how we could speak of Jesus as the Christ. My thinking could be translated into a series of writings that were part of a community engaged in revising its identity.

But Protestants also wanted to hear about these and other questions in their own terms. I have come to work and teach both as a Catholic among Catholics and as a Christian among Christians. Today I teach simultaneously at Garrett-Evangelical Theological Seminary, an institution that amalgamates the Methodist and Evangelical United Brethren traditions, and at the graduate program in religious studies at Mundelein College, a Roman Catholic institution. Previous to this I taught for ten years at a black seminary, the school of religion at Howard University (1966–76). I have also had visiting appointments at various other Catholic and Protestant institutions, as well as speaking engagements throughout the country. I have encountered American Christianity in much of its variety.

Being a Catholic Christian means, for me, being an ecumenical Christian. I identify myself as a Christian in terms of what I would call the "prophetic-messianic core" of biblical faith. This I see as the norm for judging both Scripture and tradition. I do not believe that Scripture is "enough" to create the content of Christian identity. The Protestant tendency to evacuate church history into the reapproximation of the Bible to one's contemporary preferences I find self-deluding.

We are a people with a history, much of it bad. But its bad parts also teach lessons that we should not forget. One understands the full dimensions of Christianity only by appropriating the whole of this history in its various traditions—East and West, Catholic and Protestant, the Magisterial and the Radical Reformations. Each tradition emphasizes a major element that others neglect. This is not exactly the Tillichian dialectic of "Protestant principle and Catholic substance," as though there were a dualism that could be apportioned to opposite communities. A living people exists through the constant fruitful interaction and reintegration of critical principles and historical tradition.

I would define Catholic Christianity as this whole ecumenical plurality. All particular churches exist within it as broken and partial sects. Even that communion which calls itself Catholic is also a partial and distorted reality. If I identify with this community first of all, it is not because it is the best, but because it is mine. The others are also mine in a somewhat lesser sense. This special claim on Catholicism does not mean that I have a special need to defend it. Rather it means that I have a special responsibility to question it. I have less of a responsibility to deal with the contradictions of Methodism, Lutheranism or Eastern Orthodoxy.

The prophetic ministry can be carried out authentically only within one's own community. It is only when we struggle with and for what we love that we speak responsibly. The more distant one's ties, the less one has a common base for critical conflict. What I have a right to say as a Catholic to Catholics is different from what I can say as a Christian to Protestants, as a sharer of biblical faith to Jews, as a religious person to Hindus. In each case we can engage in fruitful communication only when we have first established the ties that bind us together in community in a way that also respects the particularity of the other. Ecumenism means a shifting of the focus from attack on others to self-criticism. For example, the only group that could appropriately criticize the pope's pastoral messages in the United States in October 1979 was not the Protestants, much less the "atheists," but the Catholics. This is as it should be.

Christians and Socialism

But the 1960s were the years not only of Catholic renewal but also of exploding social consciousness in America. I, like others in that "generation," became intensely involved in the civil rights movement in the south and urban north, in the antiwar movement and in feminism. I experienced these issues not as a series of alternating commitments but as an expanding consciousness of the present human social dilemma. This dilemma appears on many levels, from the intrapersonal and interpersonal questions of identity and relationship to the social, economic and ecological systems that we construct to incarnate human life in expanding networks. The pathology of unjust and distorted relationships takes different forms on different levels. But one can understand the ramifications of one such relationship, such as racism or sexism, only by tracing it in relation to the others.

I have gradually developed a methodology of analysis which I share with a community of thinkers who would identify themselves as both Christians and socialists. This means that, even when speaking of a particular issue, such as sexism, I am concerned to situate this issue in its interconnections with class, race and economic structures. This means also that I relate the critique of social pathology and the lifting up of social alternatives to the biblical prophetic-messianic tradition. This does not mean that the biblical heritage is just a parallel language for saying the same thing. Rather it is a way of grounding the whole struggle in order to give it both greater faith and endurance and better resources to criticize its own pathology than would be the case with a secular social analysis. But I believe that socialism and biblical faith are not for two different communities, one secular and the other religious, but for the same community, the human community, divided between its ambivalent reality and its hope for salvation.

Although many social critics have taken America as the particular scapegoat for contemporary evils, I have rejected anti-Americanism. If I criticize America more severely, it is again because it is my own, not because it is worse. I find it unhelpful and self-righteous to gorge oneself on self-loathing and to establish an imaginary relationship with foreign "guerrillas." If Americans are to relate social and religious criticism authentically to themselves, they have first to take responsibility for who they are. This means finding the points at which the American tradition of religion and politics can provide a positive base for change. For example, we should not reject the dearly won tradition of civil democracy but should expand its logic to include economic democracy in a way that can speak to the American conscience. It is at this point that I have disagreed with some of the more apocalyptic or countercultural critics on the New Left.

A Feminist Analysis

My concern for feminism has been long-standing but never exclusive. I have wished to ask which feminist perspective is most adequate to address the problem of sexism. Yet feminists fear the conflict between the desire for internal criticism and the need to avoid acrimonious factionalism. Feminism in the United States spans a broad ideological spectrum. Civil-libertarian feminism is primarily concerned with "equal rights"—i.e., equal access of women to the public world of work, power and education. This feminism doesn't question the economic system within which it seeks these equal rights. Another, much smaller group of feminists is made up of socialists who link feminism with fundamental changes in the economic relation of home and work, and the class structure of paid labor. A third feminism is countercultural. It is concerned more with radical changes in symbolic consciousness and sexual identities.

There are also religious counterparts to these positions—evangelical and liberal Christian feminists and socialist Christian feminists. Radical cultural feminists believe that God the Father should be rejected in favor of a revived religion of the Goddess. Distinct feminisms appear in different ethnic and religious contexts—black feminism, Chicana feminism, Jewish feminism and (let us hope) Muslim feminism.

Feminist ecumenism is no easier to establish than Christian ecumenism, especially because feminists are forming an identity in an embattled relation to dominant institutions. My view is that none of these feminisms are "wrong." Although women as a whole are marginated by sex, they also exist in relation to males of every class, race and religion. This means that feminism necessarily must take a number of specific forms in different contexts. A feminism that deals only with equal rights or only with sexual orientation is valid in its context. But an adequate feminist analysis must embrace the whole spectrum of the female condition in such a way as to take into account the different situations of non-Christian women, working-class women, black women, married women, etc. Ideological conflict comes from absolutizing a particular limited context and drawing dogmatic conclusions; i.e., "only lesbians are truly feminists," "feminists can't be Christians," or "feminism is a white, middle-class women's problem."

In terms of religious feminism, I have been critical of an evangelical feminism whose proponents believe that they can solve the problem with better translation and exegesis but cannot reckon with serious ideological and moral error in Scripture and tradition. On the other hand, I find the "rejectionist" wing of feminist spirituality engaged in serious distortions and pretensions. Although biblical religion is sexist, it is not reducible to sexism alone! It has also been dealing with human issues, such as estrangement and oppression and the hope for reconciliation and liberation. It has been doing this on male terms, failing to apply the same critique to women. Biblical feminists use these same liberating principles of the biblical tradition. But they make the principles say new things by applying them to sexism.

I believe that countercultural feminists delude themselves when they hope that somewhere there is a "pure" feminist religion or tradition from which one can overthrow "patriarchy." All inherited culture, including the texts of goddess religion, has been biased in favor of men. Therefore, everywhere we must be engaged in a version of the same critique of culture. We must be able to claim the critical principles of every tradition and also to find how to transform the tradition by applying these principles to sexism. This means that our relation to every inherited tradition must be dialectical.

Finally, and most important, feminism must aim at a new community of mutuality for women and men, not a rejectionist community of women that impugns the humanity of men. This latter stance I regard not as a radical but as an immature position. That humiliated people succumb to desires for revenge is understandable; it is "only human." But it is not what I want to call "feminist ethics"!

If I were to define a common thread of thought and action that runs through the various issues, it would be that of dialectical methodology. A dialectical methodology seeks to be both radical and catholic in such a way that the radical side is not just an "attack," but the critical word of the tradition itself to judge, transform and renew it in new and more humanizing ways for all of us.

JOSÉ MÍGUEZ-BONINO

For Life and Against Death: A Theology That Takes Sides

I must confess that the question of how my mind has changed is one that has never exercised me much. The reason may perhaps be that, like most theologians from the so-called Third World, I have never set out to develop a theological program or to articulate an all-encompassing system. Rather I have spoken or written as questions came up, as issues were pressed upon me by circumstances or requests. Consistency or logical development has never been a conscious objective.

A Necessary Self-Examination
Occasionally, others have called my attention to changes or developments in my thinking. An American doctoral student announced that he identified three distinct stages in my theological development, moving from a church-centered to a world-centered theology. Perhaps he is right! An erstwhile colleague used to tell me that the decisive break in my thought occurred in 1968, at the time of the popular uprisings in Argentina against the military dictatorship of Onganía. Even more precisely, he timed it with the death in Rosario of a student killed by the police. He contended that my theology had since become more militant and political, that it had broken away from the captivity of a self-contained theological universe and had accepted the challenge of historicity. I had never intended to live in a purely theological universe—but, again, perhaps he is right!

My wife—who is usually right—tells me that what I have consistently tried to do is simply to reread and explain the Bible: "Questions, issues and challenges have changed," she says, "but at bottom you remain what you have always been: a preacher bound to his text." I hope she is right this time!

Only once, in 1974, as I was preparing a series of evangelistic talks, I consciously raised for myself the question of the consistency of my thinking or, more deeply, of the unity of my life. As I pondered for some hours, this is the conclusion I reached:

> When someone turns 50 and begins to view his life as something already defined and determined, like a well-traveled road, he begins to ask a question with some urgency: Can I really consider my life a unity? If I look at it objectively and dispassionately, I must answer: "I am not sure that it is like that." There are so many disconnections, so many gaps, so many dead-end streets! How many times did I have to tear out the page and start again? My intention of a few months ago to write an article on the development of my thought, another request which I finally turned down, renewed the impression: after I revised some things I had written at least two decades ago, how many inconsistencies, how many indecisions, how many starts and stops there were! [*Room to Be People* (Fortress, 1980), p. 25].

It is now again an external stimulus, the request that I write this article, that forces the perhaps necessary self-examination which I would hardly have undertaken otherwise.

Neither Despair Nor Indignation

Obviously, one has to begin with world events, and more particularly those in Latin America, which give the background—nay, which enter constitutively (and this is perhaps already a major shift in my thinking)—into theological reflection. The horizon has progressively darkened throughout the world in the past decade. On my continent, fragile hopes for a peaceful social and political transformation were dashed to pieces in Chile, in Uruguay, in Argentina and in Bolivia. The brutal regimes inspired by "national security" ideology have imposed their visible police repression and their relentless economic policies over two-thirds of the continent. The people of Nicaragua have paid an unbelievable price for a small and precarious space of freedom. In Brazil, El Salvador, Argentina, Guatemala and elsewhere in Latin America the church mourns and celebrates its martyrs.

I have become more and more convinced that neither despair nor mere moral indignation is the right response to this situation. What is happening before our eyes is a revelation, the "unmasking" of "the logic of death" in the economic-socio-political order in which we live. Awareness of this fact came to me as I was reading Milton Friedman's "theory of population" ("the production of human beings is to be regarded as if it were a deliberative economic choice determined by the balancing of returns and costs") and his distinction between "human capital" and "nonhuman capital" (that distinction being hard to predict so long as "social arrangements" grant some human freedom—should we say, so long as life remains to some extent human?) (*Price Theory* [Aldine, 1976], pp. 210–211). My quarrel is not with Friedman; it is with the logic of the system which he so clearly and consistently interprets. Life has been made finally only a function of the economic process.

As the economist-theologian Franz Hinkelammert cogently argues, the human subject vanishes and only the "fetish" (capital? property? the economic laws?) remains in control. Repression, torture, disappearances, the withdrawal of social, educational and health services, the cultural or physical genocide of native Indians, the suppression of all expressions of public opinion—these are not the result of the whim or the cruelty of bloodthirsty tyrants: they are "the necessary social cost" of "freedom." It is the sacrifice that the highest god, "the economic laws," demands.

I am aware that the logic of this "compressed" argument will not be self-evident to many readers from the affluent world. In any case, I was not invited to change their minds, but only to explain mine. May I suggest, however, that a meditation on "the unavoidability of unemployment," "the mystery of inflation," the escalation of the programs of defense and the "need" to cut down on social and assistance programs could be a healthy exercise also for theologians?

In any case, it is this insight that has come to define the framework within which I try to do theology. Many things are complex, but a basic thing seems clear: we are faced with a total system of death, a threat to all life and to the whole life. It is our Christian privilege and duty to witness concretely and unhesitantly, with all the resources we have, to God's creative and redemptive concern for life and against death! This conviction is not the result of some theological deduction. It is a commitment (shall I use the beautiful and daring Pauline word "discernment"?) that a growing number of Christians in Latin America and elsewhere have assumed—or rather, that has been forced on us, we trust, by the Spirit. We cannot bracket it out of our theological reflection.

God Has Chosen Sides

I can express this same point in a different way, one which also corresponds to my experience and studies in the '70s. The insights derived from the social sciences (particularly from social psychology, studies on the meaning and operation of ideology, and the structuralist study of the functions of language) and observations of the role played by religious language, ideas and symbols in our past and present history combine to give us an acute awareness of the unavoidable social impact of theological thinking. It is not enough, therefore, that we "enunciate the correct doctrine"; we are responsible for "the correct social operation" of that doctrine. There is no socially and politically neutral theology; in the struggle for life and against death, theology must take sides. I have to ask myself: What is my "social location" as theologian? Whose interests and concerns am I serving? Whose perspective on reality, whose experience am I adopting? (And, since it is a conflict, against whom—temporarily and conditionally, but no less resolutely—am I struggling?) In this sense, my friend is right in saying that my theology has become (contradicting my temperament) more militant.

Let it be understood: theology is not the main subject of the struggle. We theologians are not the avant-garde of "the new society." It is the struggle of the people (particularly the struggle of the poor) for their life. Moreover, it is not we who "theologize" this struggle. God himself has chosen sides—he has chosen to liberate the poor by delivering them from their misery and marginality, and to liberate the rich by bringing them down from their thrones. Christians and churches are invited to take the side of the poor, to claim solidarity with them in their struggle. And theology comes at the rear guard, as a reflection, as a help to rethink and deepen (and thus perhaps, also, if we are faithful, to correct and enrich) a commitment already undertaken as an act of obedience. To accept being simply this kind of theologian and to rejoice in it is the lesson that some of us have been trying—not always successfully—to learn during these past years.

Methodological Questions

Naturally I was not trained or conditioned for this kind of reflection. Like most of my fellow professors of the Third World, I was trained and destined to be a second-rate academic theologian (this is neither an accusation nor a sign of modesty: it is the simple recognition that we do not have the time, the infrastructure, the "milieu" or the "market"—even if we had the intelligence and the will—to pursue the rigorous course of the "developed" academic scholar). We found much in the resources of academic theology that was of value. The rediscovery of the Old Testament's historicity, and particularly of the way in which the old traditions were reread and reinterpreted for new situations; the breakthrough in Roman Catholic theology at the time of Vatican II; the birth of "political theology" in Europe—these and many other developments were of great help. But we were searching for a new way of doing theology, one that could begin at the point where our basic experience lay: with the struggle of the poor and the commitment of Christians to it.

For me it was very important to realize—of course, we all knew it all the time, but seldom thought about it—that modern academic theology, with its particular methods, was just one of the ways in which the church had thought through its faith. There was the "episcopal theology" which began with the burning issues in the life of the church in the early centuries; there was the spiritual theology of the mystics; there was free meditation commenting on Scripture in early medieval theology. This awareness brought about a great freedom to profit gratefully from the great riches of modern academic theology but to look at it as a time-bound product of an age, a place and a social class which need not be taken as universally normative.

To be sure, the questions still remained. Latin American theological production has been concerned largely with methodological questions during the past decade. As social sciences took the place of philosophy as the privileged method for interpreting human experience, new questions emerged: How should we use these sciences? Were they "auxiliary" or "constitutive" in theology? How did they affect our hermeneutics—both of Scripture and of history? How were we to choose between differing and conflicting interpretations? How was the question of "ideology" to be faced?

Although no one would claim that these questions have been sufficiently answered, I have no doubt that the joint work of a number of Catholic and Protestant theologians (here I must bear witness to the joy, the deep fellowship, the mutual support which has characterized our work, often in difficult situations) has helped to clarify some issues. This is not the place to enter into a detailed discussion of these questions. But I would like simply to indicate some of the main convictions and perspectives which I have begun to articulate during the past ten years or so.

Reflecting on Basic Motifs

In the first place, I am more and more convinced, after the first explorations and uncertainties, that theology must remain theology through and through. It will best fulfill its vocation in the struggle for liberation by retaining its specificity and refusing to dissolve its fundamental epistemological principle—it is a knowledge of faith rooted in God's self-revelation, centered and fulfilled in Jesus Christ. Moreover, this basis must be explored and articulated in its full trinitarian dimension. The living triune God is the only reality from which we can face the complex social, political and economic issues which a theology of liberation must address if it wants to be meaningful for the life and witness of the churches and Christians in our time and situation. This is the service which we can render and our only justification as theologians.

How, then, shall we articulate this relation? Is there a theologically responsible way of rereading the biblical testimony from within our present situation? How can the theologian bring out this "reserve of meaning" (as my colleague Croatto calls it) in the biblical stories without arbitrarily reading into them one's own ideology? Catholic theologians, relying on an old tradition, emphasize the "sensus fidelium" and, as one listens to the living response to the text in the Bible study of the "basis" or "popular ecclesial communities" (reflected, for instance in Ernesto Cardenal's *Gospel in Solentiname*), one becomes convinced of the truth that Jesus himself celebrated: "I thank you, Father . . . because you have hidden these things from the learned and powerful, and have revealed them to the little ones."

At the same time, as a Protestant, I look for other "intrinsic" controls. And I have come to the conclusion that the articulation of the biblical witness in terms of our situation has to be mediated by a deep consideration of basic biblical themes or "motifs," such as peace (shalom), justice, love, hope and solidarity. I am aware of the danger of falling back into an idealistic ethics. We must be on our guard, to be sure, but I don't think that this is for us a great temptation. If we keep the reflection on these basic motifs closely bound with the story of God's acts and with our concrete situation, I think it can enrich and give orientation to our commitment.

Sharpening the Tools

Then there is the use of socioanalytical tools. I find it difficult to understand that theologians in a tradition which oozes philosophy through all its pores feel free to warn us solemnly of the "ideological" danger in the use of the social sciences! For many of us it has been a painful and at times frustrating exercise to go "back to school" and sit at the feet of the social scientists, trying to understand their categories of analysis, to evaluate the results, to distinguish the different orientations, and to try to relate this knowledge with integrity to our theological work. But it has been a fruitful exercise in which a true and open fellowship has emerged. Interdisciplinary work born in a common commitment and carried out in mutual respect is now a reality for Latin American theology. We theologians should not forget that, after all, it was the social scientists' reflection on "dependence and liberation" which awakened us to a basic *biblical* motif!

There are two points in relation to the question of "social analysis" which we have had to face. One has to do with "theoretical thinking." Not seldom is it pointed out that some of our work moves at a level of "abstraction." For most of us this is an existential question because we are engaged at the same time in pastoral and "academic" work (jacks of all trades!) and would not be ready to withdraw from either.

For my part, I am convinced that theology has to find expression in different forms and styles, all of them necessary but no one absolutely normative: the impassioned word of the prophet (witness many of the episcopal letters in our continent); the spontaneous, concrete response of the basis-community; the spiritual meditation of the mystic (Ernesto Cardenal's poems or Arturo Paoli's meditations on the Gospels), *and* the rigorous "theoretical" work of the academic. We are concerned with the *unity* of all of this, not with a reduction.

Now the academic work has a subordinate place: it depends on and draws from the praxis and experience of the community, and aims at serving it through the analysis of this experience and praxis. It is at this point that the theologian must try to sharpen the critical (socioanalytical and hermeneutical) instruments of the trade. Theory is one's business! Sloppy and careless talk and alienated and irrelevant theory are the Scylla and Charybdis between which one has to walk.

Christians and Marxists

During these years I have had to face many misunderstandings—some genuine, some contrived—concerning the relation of liberation theology to Marxism. In Latin America, moreover, more than academic status is at stake in this issue. I have tried to clarify some aspects of this relation (see *Christians and Marxists* [Eerdmans, 1976]).

Let me try to express in a few sentences not the substantive question but my personal attitude. I have never felt attracted to Marxism as a system; neither have I felt inclined to enroll in any anti-Marxist crusade. Since my youth (in which I was attracted to the Argentine socialist—non-Marxist—party) I have believed that certain elements of the Marxist economic and social analysis were correct. I have never experienced the *Entdeckungsfreude* (joy of discovery) that my friend and colleague Jürgen Moltmann thought he had spotted in some of us. I have more and more come to think in terms of a long humanist-socialist tradition, with early Christian and Hellenic roots, which has developed in the modern world, in which Marx has played an important—even decisive—part, but which he has neither created nor fulfilled.

In this sense I firmly believe that we must—now with Moltmann's words—"demythologize" the Marx question. On this basis I have found it possible to work together with Marxists and others—on questions of human rights, for instance—with clarity and mutual respect.

I must say it directly: this socialist option—as Gustavo Gutiérrez defines it, the social appropriation of the means of production, of the political decision, and of human freedom—is the immediate context of my theological work. It is not an absolute, not an object of faith, but simply a sociopolitical decision (a lucid one, I hope) which concretely defines my Christian obedience in the world at this time. Theologically, I think it is a historical project partially and ambiguously but really and intrinsically related to God's Kingdom, and therefore to my Christian hope. The gospel does not stand or fall with the correctness of this view. But my theology does. After all, if the Century authorizes us to change our minds every ten years, why should we claim any greater permanence for our theology!

LETTY M. RUSSELL

Bread Instead of Stone

In reflecting back over the past 30 years of my ministry in the church, I find that my style of thought and commitment has not changed a great deal. Throughout my ministry in the United Presbyterian Church—both lay and ordained—I have been concerned with the way in which God's "good gifts" can be experienced as *bread* instead of *stone.*

Overcoming Dualism

The structures of the church and of society often undercut the reality of this gospel message, and the good gifts God offers to the children of God turn to stone (Matt. 9–11). Not only blacks, the poor, women and all of society's misfits, but even the beneficiaries of the establishment find themselves with institutions that are no longer plausible expressions of their faith, and with faith that no longer shapes their lives and institutions. The "bread of life" offered in the suffering love of Christ has turned to stone in a world hungry for true bread and compassion. To find ways of living and working with others so that God's gifts may be experienced as *good* has been, and continues to be, the evangelical motif of my ministry.

My style of thought and commitment continues to be not only evangelical but also holistic. In my work as educator, pastor, bureaucrat and theologian, I have continued to seek out ways of overcoming dualistic patterns of thought and action. In trying to overcome the dualism of experience and tradition I have found that "acting one's way into thinking" is a helpful form of theological reflection. Therefore, I continue to value experience and action in ministry as a source of questions and challenge to accustomed patterns of reflection.

My theological perspective is rooted in the neo-Reformed tradition of biblical theology, and this rootage tends to *code* much of my experience with the interpretive bias of this tradition. At the same time I have found myself continually *challenging* this interpretation of reality in the light of my life experiences. As my life has changed, the questions I work on have changed. Thus the particular context of my life experience provides a key to understanding how my mind has (and has not) changed in the past decade.

The year 1969–70 was a watershed one for my life and ministry. As a stereotyped example of what Gail Sheehy calls the "Deadline Decade," I moved into my 40s with a re-evaluation of my ministry and a shifting back to some of my earlier life patterns. In that year I finished my doctorate and moved from my pastoral life and work in the East Harlem Protestant Parish to become a professor of theology, first at Manhattan College and then at Yale Divinity School. In the same year I was married to the Dutch theologian Hans Hoekendijk, who was teaching world Christianity at Union Theological Seminary in New York. I moved from a ghetto created by poverty and racism to a largely white, middle-class academic ghetto. My work for the elimination of racism was broadened to include activities related to the elimination of sexism. In 1969 I was living out my response to God's call to freedom and service as an inner-city pastor. In 1970 my response was lived out as a feminist theologian.

Naming the Struggle

The story of this past decade is not hard to document, for print is one of the media of my ministry, and my struggle to become a feminist and remain a Christian was shared with many others who were on the same journey toward freedomland. The titles of books written in the past ten years point to my major efforts at naming that struggle.

While working as a part-time religious consultant for the National Board of the YWCA, I reflected on ways to relate the Christian faith to participation in social change. In 1972, while teaching with my husband at the United Theological College in Bangalore, India, I finished a study book for the YWCA designed to help women in Christian organizations join with others in the process of liberation. That book, *Ferment of Freedom*, came out of a process of conscientization for myself and others as various groups of women tested the materials over and over. The fermenting process of group thought, discussion and action was, I hope, helpful in loosening some of the personal and social shackles of women's lives.

Following the lead of Paulo Freire, I was concerned that persons learn not only to perceive the social, political, economic and ecclesial contradictions in their lives, but also to take steps together with others to change them. Already in terms of my educational praxis I was trying to find out how the "revolution of rising expectations" affecting all parts of our globe could be shared and acted upon in ways that developed more human values.

This search for human liberation soon led me to articulate my commitment to the human struggle against oppression in relation to various types of liberation theology. In 1974 I wrote *Human Liberation in a Feminist Perspective—A Theology*. Here I came to describe liberation as an attempt to reflect on the experience of oppression in the light of our participation in God's liberating actions in the creation of a more human society. I tried to show that, while each theology is contextual, the style and themes of many black, Latin American and feminist theologies have a great deal in common.

This was and continues to be a key issue for my theology, for feminist theology cannot talk of a "new house of freedom" unless that house includes all those groaning to be free (Rom. 8:22). A feminist is one who advocates equality of the sexes in every culture, class and race. The particular form of feminist theology with which I feel most at home is that which continues in a historical/biblical framework and attempts to reflect on the experience of sexist oppression in the light of participation in God's liberating actions.

The style of liberation theologies provides opportunity for church renewal because these theologies encourage all people, not just professional theologians, to participate in the process of sharing the actions and thoughts of their lives. This style of doing theology is a collective attempt to live out faith, and all are invited, especially those who find themselves in communities of struggle for a more human society. In the commitment to justice there is a sharing of God's bias toward the poor and the marginalized who listen for the good news (Matt. 11:15). Such a style is rooted in concrete contexts or situations and moves inductively out of those situations to understand the meaning of God's summons to journey with others toward the New Creation. Critical reflection and action are used as a continuing process of discerning the Way.

Partnership

In 1976 I edited a book called *The Liberating Word: A Guide to Non-Sexist Interpretation of the Bible*. It also represented a key aspect of my naming the struggle, for here I confessed once again that it was the biblical witness to Christ and to God's intention for New Humanity that was the center of my faith. At the same time I shared with my sisters in raising critical and painful questions about the patriarchal perspective of biblical and church tradition which is reinforced in the use of noninclusive language. The Word of God is liberating when by the power of the Holy Spirit it comes alive again in our hearts and actions.

But often the Word of God has been spoken through the words of men and interpreted in a male-centered and androcentric way. Thus this Word needs to be "liberated" so that it might become the "bread of life" rather than a stone around the necks of those who are marginalized by the tradition. Just as non-Western cultures must seek to liberate the white, Western interpretations of Scripture and theology so that they are heard anew in different cultures and subcultures, women must seek to liberate the interpretation of God's Word from male bias.

In every culture, language plays an important role in addressing problems of discrimination in church and society. We cannot be true to the gospel message if we preach it in ways that often ignore large portions of the human race. Our words reflect the nature of reality as we see it, and they can be powerful tools, either for oppression or liberation. As we seek to heed the call of Christ to freedom and unity, the way we use language is an indicator of our commitment to being partners in the full human community. The fact that it is difficult to change is no excuse, for it is relatively easy to learn new forms of language. What is difficult is to change the structures of reality that they both mirror and shape.

Partnership has emerged as a key area of my reflection in the past decade. In a world falling apart, how do we relate together as oppressors and oppressed? How do we as Christians find ways to live now, as if we really are "one in Christ Jesus" (Gal. 3:28)? In East Harlem I saw the difficulty of responding to the koinonia-creating presence of Christ in the midst of differences of race and class.

This difficulty is even more apparent when we broaden the naming of that struggle to include the relationships between women and men in church and society. Having worked on issues of human liberation, I wanted to "keep the rumor going" that there is life after liberation. Thus it was important to re-examine the way God is partner with Godself and with all creation, and the way in which we share this partnership through Jesus Christ.

In describing koinonia as a new focus of relationship in the common history of Jesus Christ that sets persons free for others, I sought to discuss how we can begin to live in free and responsible relationships now, as groups of two, three or 5,000. This was particularly important to me because I had lost my husband through a sudden heart attack and shared the pain of many others who suddenly find the fabric of their lives torn to shreds. In 1979 *The Future of Partnership* was a way of celebrating my partnership with Hans. At the same time, it was an effort to forge an eschatological perspective that might open up a more creative approach to partnership for those caught up in life styles not even imagined by the writers of the Genesis creation stories.

Continuing Theological Themes

It is quite apparent even in this brief description of issues that have preoccupied my mind and life in this decade that the issues themselves are deeply coded by my past experience and the continuity of my theological perspective. My commitment to an ongoing partnership in the education and conscientization process stems from my life as an educator and pastor and my earlier writings on education as participation in God's mission. My concern for the renewal of theology and the church so that persons can hear the good news and experience it in their lives was part of my work for renewal as a member of the East Harlem Protestant Parish and of the World Council of Churches working committees on the Missionary Structures of the Congregation and on Christians Within Changing Institutions.

The biblical promises helped to make sense of the suffering of an inner-city ghetto and of the civil rights struggle, and they continue to help make sense in my life and ministry of teaching. The Bible has never had "all the answers," and therefore it is not surprising that it brings many problems to feminists of faith. Yet it continues to be a liberating way of naming my struggle as part of God's saving purpose. Nor are my attempts to overcome problems of dualism and pluralism without precedent, for I have a bias toward the world and myself in wanting things to be whole. This is a bias that I share with many of my sisters and not a few of my brothers.

Yet these theological traditions continue to be broken open and mined for new riches and shifted in new directions. Already I have moved into the '80s with a sense of excitement about what new things God might have in store for my life and mind. Some of the areas that I am presently exploring reflect this latest search.

In the area of education I continue to reflect on my own praxis as a professional theological educator and on the experience and questions of others in this field in order to discover how persons of all ages can share in a process of learning to become partners. Having tried to understand the meaning of liberating partnership more clearly, I am still left with the next question: How do we become partners; how do we educate for partnership? After a number of years of trying to educate for partnership in seminary classroom, church committee, worship, workshop, study group, lecture and social-change organization, I still have not answered that question.

In an effort to research my own question and to discover new clues I am writing a book on education for partnership. Perhaps by the time I am finished I might have more clues, or at least a new set of questions. Partnership is essentially a gift of God's Spirit. For that reason, the basic educational process is to invite persons to be partners so that they may discover this gift along with others who are seeking the gift of partnership. Yet often the structures of the churches and educational institutions mirror the domination and subordination of society. Thus a "new house of freedom" needs constantly to be built where there is space for growth and response to the Spirit. In such a space all persons would be only temporarily unequal rather than finding themselves in rigid roles of what Jean Baker Miller calls "permanent inequality."

Hope for the Struggle

A second area of exploration is that of continual renewal of communities of struggle. The communities, whether they be Christian or not, need a strong sense of "hope against hope" and a vision of new life that informs the day-to-day struggle (Rom. 4:18). Perhaps the best way to describe this concern is to speak of it as the search for what Gustavo Gutiérrez calls "spirituality of liberation." How do we "keep on keeping on" the freedom road in a world of unfreedom? How do we avoid the danger of sell-out or burn-out?

Some people, in seeing that I persist in writing about partnership in a world where some partners are always more equal than others, tend to think that I myself have sold out, crying "peace, peace" where there is no peace. Yet we cannot anticipate the meaning of liberation and educate for that liberation if we do not dare to image that which we seek. This very vision may be what sustains us when we would otherwise burn out or grow weary. In a world that is hazardous to the health of all liberation struggles we have to keep on learning to develop a spirituality that concretely anticipates God's intention of partnership for all creation.

A third area of ever-growing interest in my life is that of eschatological methodology in approaching questions of biblical interpretation and contemporary issues. I made a beginning in this area by discussing partnership from the perspective of God's intention for New Creation rather than from the perspective of Old Creation. I understand this eschatological hermeneutic as a constant "hermeneutic of suspicion" in which one questions the text and context of the writers and listeners in the light of emerging questions and shared stories from the perspective of the oppressed. Such a hermeneutic is a process of questioning our actions and our society in the light of the biblical promise of New Creation. The end of history is seen as the newness of creation breaking into life so that we discover signs of God's "new thing" now in our lives (Isa. 43:18–19).

Such a perspective may well yield results in key areas of contemporary theological investigation. One such area shared by feminists and dogmatic theologians alike is that of theological anthropology. We have come far enough in investigation of that area in feminist theology to know that the "doctrine of man" has been of, for and by men, and that the exalted view of men as "a little lower than the angels" (Ps. 8:5, KJV) has had disastrous effects on all that is "not fully human," such as the natural order, "underdeveloped" peoples, women and children. But what is the alternative to such anthropology? Certainly one might be that of imaging new humanity eschatologically as part of God's New Creation. This image is one that might inform our lives now if we took the words of Paul seriously: "When anyone is united in Christ, there is a new world, the old order has gone and a new order has already begun" (II Cor. 5:17, NEB).

A final area of continuing interest for me is the need to develop new methodologies for doing theology in a pluralistic world. My experience in the Faith and Order commissions of the World Council of Churches and the National Council of Churches has led me to realize over and over that there is a missing link in the way contextual theology is related to doctrinal theology. We proceed to examine the "hope that is in us" in divergent nations, denominations and cultures and then try to get a common denominator from the doctrine that fits all the stories.

It would seem that we need to develop methods of interpretation that move from the diversity of the stories to shared story in the common history of Jesus Christ, rather than moving directly from stories to doctrine. In this way we might be able to serve the cause of unity in Christ while honoring the integrity of concrete experiences of Christ's presence. An important aspect of this dialogue about ways of sharing the results of both inductive and deductive thinking is the need for sharing experiences in developing a "pedagogy for the oppressor" in which those who find their perspective about the Good News limited by interests of class, race, sex, sexual preference, age or nationality can be supported in their own process of conscientization. This will be of crucial importance in the coming years for those who seek to live out what Marie Augusta Neal calls a "sociotheology of letting go."

The Continuing Journey

Certainly I have changed in the past ten years, in the midst of my grace-filled yet often hectic life. I have discovered the way that partnership can be the source of one's very life. This way of partnership with God and others has given me a sense of strength, openness and confidence because I am loved, yet that very openness seems to make me ever more vulnerable. In experiencing death and sickness I have discovered the way pain drives me to greater depth of commitment to Christ and to greater patience with my own limitations and failings.

I think my mind has changed as well. In a process of continued conversion, I discover that God's Word has managed to break through to me as a feminist of faith. Yet as I grow older I discover that there is much in my mind that doesn't change. Now in my 50th year I am often happy to recognize ideas, people and events as old friends. I hope to continue to celebrate both the metanoia and the continuity through the next decade and beyond. And in the continuing journey I hope to share God's love as the "bread of life" for all persons.

JAMES H. CONE

The Gospel and the Liberation of the Poor

What has the gospel of God to do with the weak and helpless and their struggle for freedom in human society? This question, the most critical issue that has shaped my theological consciousness, first achieved its importance in the particularity of the black religious experience during my early childhood in Bearden, Arkansas. Although the formulation of the question was not always precise, the everyday experience of black suffering, arising from black people's encounter with the sociopolitical structures controlled by whites, created in my consciousness a radical conflict between the claims of faith on the one hand and the reality of the world on the other.

Being Christian in a Racist Society

I remember discussing with my brother Cecil this conflict between the Christian faith and black suffering, and no rational explanation seemed to satisfy either of us. "If God is good," we asked, "and also capable of accomplishing his will, why then do black people suffer so much at the hands of white people? What was the reason for black slavery and our subsequent oppression? What does God plan to do about righting the wrongs inflicted upon our people?" These and similar questions occupied much of our intellectual reflection as we attempted to reconcile the reality of our everyday experience with our faith in Jesus Christ.

The conflict between faith and suffering was exacerbated by the fact that most of the brutality inflicted upon black people was done by white persons who also called themselves Christians. Whites who humiliated blacks during the week went to church on Sunday and prayed to the God of Moses and of Jesus. Although blacks and whites expressed their faith in their separate worship services in quite different ways, the verbal content of their faith seemed similar. That was why many blacks asked: How could whites be Christian and yet do such horrible things to black people? And why does God permit white people to do evil things in the name of Jesus Christ? During my childhood in Bearden, the exclusion of black people from white churches was the most obscene contradiction that I could imagine.

Viewed from the experience of black people, life in Bearden during the 1940s and early '50s was not easy. In this small town of 800 whites and 400 blacks, I encountered the white American reality that would prove decisive for my theological development. It was not that whites in Bearden were worse than whites in similar towns in Arkansas or other southern states. The opposite is more likely the case. Bearden is important because it happened to be the geographical context in which the ugliness of racism was clearly revealed to me, and I knew that I had to struggle against it. Since the church was so much a part of the whole of black life, I had to ask: What has the gospel of God to do with the extreme limits placed on the black community? Explicitly or implicitly every black Christian had to ask that question. There was no way to avoid it, because the contradiction to which the question pointed was inherent in the attempt to be Christian in a racist society.

The Problem of Evil

My preoccupation with the conflict between faith and suffering deepened when I began my philosophical studies at Shorter and Philander Smith colleges. Professors James and Alice Boyack of Philander Smith made philosophical issues concrete, and I wrote several papers on the problem of evil and suffering. At Shorter and Philander Smith, I developed the self-confidence that I could think—a discovery not encouraged among blacks by most intellectual structures controlled by whites.

Although my studies at those two schools introduced me to the scope and depth of Western thought on the issue of evil, the way in which the problem was defined was quite different from its definition in the black church. The weight of the problem of evil in the black church was not located primarily in terms of God's need to justify himself in view of the presence of suffering in the world. That God is both good and powerful is taken for granted in the black church, and if any inexplicable contradiction emerges, black Christians always appeal to God's mystery, quoting the often repeated lines, "God moves in a mysterious way." They really believe Paul's saying that "all things work together for good to them that love God" (Rom. 8:28, KJV).

What then is the heart of the contradiction between faith and suffering in the context of black life? The contradiction is found not in God but in white people who claim to be Christian and yet oppose the sociopolitical equality of black people. This contradiction was blatant in the south, but it was found also in other parts of the U.S.

Institutional Racism in the North

When I graduated with a Bachelor of Arts degree from Philander Smith and was accepted at Garrett Theological Seminary in Evanston, Illinois (now Garrett-Evangelical), I was a little naïve, for I was sure that things would be different. I had internalized the myth that blacks were treated equally "up north," but that myth was demolished for me in less than one day in Evanston and at Garrett. Although racism at Garrett and in Evanston was not as obvious as in Arkansas, I believe that it was much more vicious, especially in terms of the structural brutality inflicted upon black dignity and self-confidence. I almost did not survive past my first quarter at Garrett, making all C's from professors who told me that I deserved less. This was a common experience for the few blacks allowed to matriculate at Garrett during the late 1950s and early '60s.

Had it not been for the confidence in my self-worth I had received from my mother and father, I am sure that the challenge at Garrett would have defeated me, as so many white institutions continue to defeat black people today. But when I remembered the extreme odds against which my father struggled in Bearden (and he had only a sixth-grade education!), that memory gave me the emotional and intellectual strength to overcome the difficulties at Garrett.

My father was self-employed, cutting logs and billets, because he refused to work at the sawmills in and around Bearden. I once asked him why he chose the uncertainty of self-employment when he could easily get a regular job at a sawmill or some other company. He quickly replied, "My son, a black man cannot be a man and also work for white people." Watching my father meet the challenge of southern racism prepared me for the challenge of northern institutional racism that I encountered at Garrett and later at Northwestern.

Despite Garrett's racism, however, I had some very good teachers there. Without the constant encouragement of William Hordern, Philip Watson and Ed Perry, I am sure that I would not have even applied for the Ph.D. program in systematic theology. They and other professors gave me the intellectual structure in which to relate Christianity and racism, even though the latter was almost never mentioned as a theological problem.

In one class I made the connection between racism and theology in a highly provocative manner, by saying to one of my professors that he was a racist, since he could easily talk about the injustice that Roman Catholics inflicted on Protestants in the 16th century, but failed to say a word against white Christians (Protestants and Catholics) who openly support black suffering in the U.S. today. There was complete silence in the classroom, followed by a sudden outburst of anger from the professor: "That's simply not true! Class dismissed!"

After that event, I realized that Garrett would not be the best context for expressing my deepest feelings about racism, if I expected to receive a Ph.D. degree from that institution. That was why I did not raise the racism issue as a theological problem, and also why I decided to write a dissertation on Karl Barth's anthropology rather than on some issue in the black community. It was not until I left Garrett and Northwestern and returned to Philander Smith to teach religion and philosophy that I began to ask more formally about the relation between faith and suffering as that contradiction is defined in the black community. What did Friedrich Schleiermacher, Adolf Harnack and Karl Barth have to do with young black students who came from the cotton fields of the south, looking to create a new future for their lives? That question was not easy to answer.

Black Power and the Gospel

Philander Smith College and the civil rights movement of the 1960s made a significant impact upon my theological development. Both made me realize that I could not avoid inquiring about the relation between the Christian faith and black people's struggle for freedom. Unfortunately, my formal training in theology did not prepare me for the investigation of this issue. Therefore, I began a disciplined reading program in the history, literature and religion of black people. When I left Philander Smith to teach at Adrian College in Michigan, I even considered returning to graduate school for a Ph.D. in literature at the University of Chicago. It seemed that such writers as Albert Camus, Jean-Paul Sartre, Richard Wright and James Baldwin could speak much more creatively than theologians about life and suffering. I discussed the possibility of my return to graduate school with Nathan Scott, Jr., who was then teaching theology and literature at the University of Chicago. It was then the summer of 1967, and before I could make the necessary arrangements for my return, 43 blacks were killed in the Detroit riot. Similar events occurred that summer in many other American cities. There was no time for me to return to graduate school. I had to say something now about God and black people's struggle for freedom. But what could I say?

The challenge to say something about God and the black liberation struggle was enhanced when Ronald Goetz (a classmate during my student years at Garrett) invited me in February 1968 to lecture at Elmhurst College, where he was teaching. I accepted his invitation and decided to lecture on the theme of "Christianity and Black Power." I attempted to demonstrate that, contrary to popular opinion, black power is not alien to the gospel. It *is* the gospel of Jesus Christ. I knew that this extreme way of expressing my point would not be accepted by white theologians and preachers who were contending that black power means reverse racism and black violence. The anticipated white rejection of my equation of Christianity and black power encouraged me to write an extended argument in its defense.

By the summer of 1968, I could no longer contain my rage. I was extremely angry with white churches and their theologians who were contending that black power was the sin of black pride and thus the opposite of the gospel. Since white theologians and preachers wrote most of the books in religion and theology, they had a great deal of power in controlling the public meaning of the gospel. During my six years of graduate work at Garrett and Northwestern, not one book written by a black person was used as required reading. Does this not suggest that only whites know what theology and the gospel are? The implication of that question consumed my whole being. I *had* to write *Black Theology and Black Power* in order to set myself free from the bondage of white theology.

The writing of *Black Theology and Black Power* (during the summer of 1968) was a deep emotional experience for me. It was a cleansing experience, because I endeavored to purge myself of any direct dependence upon my white theological mentors. I am not sure how much I succeeded, but I delighted in exposing the blindness created by their own racism. For me, it was a choice between satisfying the theological values of white people's racism and saying a word of encouragement for the black freedom struggle. I was very much aware of the possible ideological distortion of the gospel in identifying it with black power, for no one can read Barth seriously and not be cognizant of that danger. But I felt that the urgency of the black situation demanded that the risk be taken.

The publication of *Black Theology and Black Power* (1969) put me in contact with an ecumenical group in the National Conference of Black Churchmen (NCBC). Through the influence of C. Eric Lincoln, I also received an invitation to teach theology at Union Theological Seminary in New York. Union and NCBC became the theological and political contexts for reflecting upon the relation between Christian theology and the black liberation struggle.

Captive of White Concepts?

My first attempt to write a systematic theology, using black liberation as the central motif, was published as *A Black Theology of Liberation* (1970). This second book was even less satisfying to many white theologians than the first one. But during this period, I did not care what whites thought about my work. I was concerned only with speaking the truth of the gospel as disclosed in the black experience of freedom. Since the writing of my first essay on "Christianity and Black Power," it had become very clear to me that the gospel was identical with the liberation of the poor from oppression. That was why I identified the gospel with black power, and the white church with the Antichrist. Although I would express each identification a little differently today, I still stand by the theological truth that gave rise to that conviction.

However, I neglected to reflect this conviction in the theological sources I used to define black theology. It appeared that I was more enslaved to white theological concepts than I realized. Charles Long, Gayraud Wilmore and other black colleagues were quick to point to this weakness. How can theology be black if the sources used for its explication are derived primarily from the white Western theological tradition? What is the relation between my definition of black theology and Karl Barth, Paul Tillich and Dietrich Bonhoeffer, all of whom were highly visible in my analysis of black theology? Is there any relation between black liberation and the cultural and theological resources used to analyze its meaning?

My black colleagues in NCBC and the Society for the Study of Black Religion (SSBR) helped me to realize more clearly that theology is not black merely because of its identification with a general concept of freedom. It is necessary for the language of theology to be derived from the history and culture of black people. The issue is whether black history and culture have anything unique to contribute to the meaning of theology. Must we assume that the meaning of theology as a discipline is limited to the definitions found in white people's reflections? In an attempt to take seriously the criticisms of my black colleagues, I wrote *The Spirituals and the Blues* (1972) and *God of the Oppressed* (1975).

Women's Experience

During the mid-1970s, two realities began to affect my theological consciousness—the women's movement and the Third World. It was impossible to teach at Union Seminary and not be deeply moved by the theological importance of women's experience in theology. The presence of the feminist consciousness among black women at Union and in the black church made it difficult to dismiss feminism as a concern of white women alone. It became very clear to me that black theology could not continue to ignore sexism and still claim to be concerned about the freedom of the oppressed. Women of all cultures have much to teach black men about theology and the human struggle to be free.

As is always the case, it is difficult for people to recognize the significance of a particular form of experience when it does not arise from their own lives. My attempt to recognize the importance of women's experience in theology is found in the classes I teach at Union, and also in a section on "Black Theology and Black Women" in *Black Theology: A Documentary History, 1966–1979*, by Gayraud S. Wilmore and James H. Cone. My earlier books ignored the issue of sexism; I believe now that such an exclusion was and is a gross distortion of the theological meaning of the Christian faith. Like racism, sexism is deeply embedded in the fabric of human cultures, and we must struggle against it if we expect to make this world a more humane place in which to live. Third World and black women have begun to make this point with increasing power and clarity, and we black men had better listen to them or we will be devoured by the revolutions that they are making.

The Impact of the Third World

In addition to the women's movement, the theological and political happenings in Africa, Asia and Latin America have had an enormous impact upon my theological perspective. When I first began to write about black theology, the particularity of black suffering in the United States was so dominant in my consciousness that I could not easily see beyond it to oppression in other parts of the world. It was not that I was completely unaware of the suffering of Third World peoples. Rather, the existential pain of black people's suffering was so much a part of my reality that I had to explore first its significance before moving to a larger dimension.

The impact of the Third World on my thinking is found in the theological resources used in my classes at Union and also in the Wilmore-Cone book, *Black Theology: a Documentary History* (see Part VI, "Black Theology and Third World Theologies"). From my reading and personal experiences in Africa, Asia and Latin America, I now know that the complexity of human oppression is much greater than I had realized, and it cannot be reduced to North American expressions of white racism.

Under the auspices of NCBC, the World Council of Churches, the Ecumenical Association of Third World Theologians (EATWOT), and the Korean Christian Church in Japan, I have visited many countries in Africa, Asia and Latin America. It is one thing to read about poverty in the Third World and quite another to see it. I had to ask: What is the relation between the struggles of black people in the U.S. and the struggles of people in the Third World? In my attempt to answer that question, I realized that racism, sexism, classism and imperialism are interrelated and thus cannot be separated.

My dialogues with Third World theologians in EATWOT and my contacts with Koreans in Japan and South Korea have been particularly important in extending my theological perspective to a global context. Since 1976 EATWOT has been sponsoring dialogues among theologians in Asia, Africa and Latin America and oppressed racial minorities in the U.S. Major conferences have been held in Tanzania (August 1976), Ghana (December 1977), Sri Lanka (January 1979) and Brazil (February 1980). Accounts of the first three conferences have been published by Orbis Books under the titles *The Emergent Gospel, African Theology en Route* and *Asia's Struggle for Full Humanity*. I have written essays from a black American perspective on Asian, African and Latin American theologies. These dialogues helped me to see more clearly the importance of class oppression and the role of U.S. imperialism in oppressing poor countries.

The Socialist Alternative

While my perspective has been enlarged through dialogues with feminist, Third World and other theologians of the poor, I would not say that it has changed radically. I still contend that the gospel is identical with the liberation of poor people from sociopolitical oppression. I have never suggested that blacks were the only poor. Instead I said that if any person attempted to do theology in North America in the 1960s and '70s but failed to speak of God's identity with the black struggle for freedom, he or she was not doing Christian theology. I still stand by that claim but now specifically include men and women in the Third World.

It has also been my contact with the Third World, especially Africa, that has led me to consider socialism as an alternative to monopoly capitalism. So long as the maximization of profit and growth is the chief regulating ideal, the gap between the rich and poor will continue to increase. We must therefore form a social arrangement that is democratic, both economically and politically. No one should control for profit those goods and services needed for human survival.

Unfortunately, most political and economic arrangements that use the terms socialism and democracy as a description of their identity do the opposite of what they claim to do. The absence of a historical model that embodies fully my political and theological imagination makes it difficult to speak meaningfully and concretely about the socialist alternative. What I do believe, to use the words of Gustavo Gutiérrez, is "the non-necessity of the present order." What is, is not supposed to be, and we are required by that conviction to project a future social order wherein all can develop to their fullest potential.

The absence of a historical model is no reason to deny the dream. Through dreams we can see what is supposed to be when what is blinds us to what *ought to be*. In my dialogues with Third World Christians, I have sought to use the creative aspects of the black Christian eschatology in order to help us to see beyond what is present to the future that is coming. I believe that my theological development will always be related to the historical projects of poor people as they struggle to build a new future not recognizable in the present world order.

ROBERT McAFEE BROWN

Starting Over: New Beginning Points for Theology

Having contributed to this series a decade ago, I thought it appropriate to start reflecting on the past decade by rereading what I had said about the previous one. That nearly proved fatal.

We are always in danger of being either mesmerized or appalled by our past prose. (I use "mesmerized" in the sense of being hypnotized or spellbound; e.g., rendered incapable of change, and thus locked into affirming once again what we affirmed back then, in order to maximize the sense of our prescience and minimize the sense of our shortsightedness. I use "appalled" in the sense of being appalled. No further comment needed.)

Although there were some personal things that happened in the '70s that I hadn't anticipated in the '60s, I was cheered to discover that some of the things that flourished in the '70s had roots that were nourished in the '60s so that there are continuities as well as changes.

But I am not going to dwell extensively on either the personal story or the continuities, for two reasons. The first is that I have recently concluded a somewhat longer exercise in sorting out the personal story. Those Who Really Care can read *Creative Dislocation–The Movement of Grace* (Abingdon, 1980), and a little exegesis of the title will say enough about the personal story for present needs. For me the '70s were a decade of personal *dislocation*—geographic (twice), psychic, financial, ideological and theological, but nevertheless *creative* despite such traumas, because I became able, after considerable effort, to see the dislocations as instances of the *movement of grace*. I discovered that being uprooted, on journey , *in via*, less "fixed" than I might choose to be, goes with the territory of trying to be part of the pilgrim people. I surely wouldn't have designed it that way had I been consulted, but I now want to be as responsive as I can, with a minimum of resistance, when an ongoing journey rather than a settled existence turns out to be the name of the game. (Hebrews 11-12:3 is pretty big for me these days.)

During the last half of the decade alone, I left Stanford University (in a bit of a huff), returned to Union Theological Seminary, left there three years later (in a bit of a huff), and am now teaching half-time at Pacific School of Religion (hopeful that the huffing is over), and excited by a chance to teach theology and ethics along with having a good chunk of time free each year to carry on a more disciplined "apostolate of the pen." The latter agenda has recreated my spirit. There is a lot of writing I want to get started before I "retire" (only halfway through the *next* decade), for I anticipate that my physical energies will begin to wane no matter how furiously the authorial juices are boiling.

The second reason I intend to dwell less on the personal story or the continuities is that the editors want stress on the *changes*, which are always more interesting than the continuities. And as I examine the changes, I discover that they really do involve some basically new directions.

A Brand-New Key

For years I lived contentedly in the world of white Anglo-Saxon theology, spruced up by such continental theology as I could get in translation. (It would never have occurred to me in those days that the adjective "continental" could modify any noun theologically save "Europe.") It was the time of Barth, Brunner, Bultmann, Berdyaev, Bonhoeffer (along with Tillich and Niebuhr, even though their inclusion spoils the alliteration). We were living in an era of giants. Who needed *new* giants? Our generation's task was to share what we had seen while riding on the giants' backs.

How wrong I was.

What I thought of as "normative theology" turned out to be parochial theology—conditioned, in ways I had never imagined, by the times and places out of which it arose. Even theologies claiming to be built on "the biblical perspective" turned out to be built on a *parochial* biblical perspective—the Bible as read from a white, male, Western, bourgeois, intellectual perspective rather than from the perspective of the biblical writers themselves, most of whom turn out to have been dark-skinned Orientals, "the poor of the land" rather than the cream of the intelligentsia.

This recognition—that my perspective was just as conditioned as everybody else's, rather than being the "norm" from which "they" (i.e., everybody else) deviated—was force-fed to me by the reality of a shrinking globe, and the recognition that while I had been listening and learning in congenial places close to my cultural home, Christians in Asia and Africa and Latin America were engaging in a theological declaration of independence from the rest of us. It meant starting all over again.

The image that has helped me in starting all over again has been the musical example of the diminished seventh chord, an image I developed in detail in a book called *Theology in a New Key* (Westminster, 1978). In writing music, I remembered in an exciting moment in 1976, composers sometimes introduce a chord called a diminished seventh, which enables them to shift quite abruptly to a different key. By means of this device they can move in unexpected directions and take their listeners by surprise. Much the same thing seems to me to have been happening in theology. We have been singing in a certain way—i.e., a North American–European way—and now, to our surprise, the song has emerged in a brand-new key, sung by a new group of people.

> Many terms have been used to describe the articulators of the theology in a new key—the "wretched of the earth," the poor, the oppressed, the marginalized, the voiceless, the exploited, the victims. Their spokespersons vary and their agendas vary: they are women, blacks, the physically and mentally handicapped, homosexuals, Asians, Latin Americans. Some of them come from Appalachia in West Virginia, others from the altiplano in eastern Peru; some live in the barrios, others in the Bowery; some are at home in Chilean *poblaciones*, others in Malaysia. . . . Their theology is being forged in conversations rather than in academic lectures; printed on mimeographed newssheets (clandestinely distributed with no return address) rather than in volumes selling for $10.95 plus tax; . . . preached in prisons as much as in chapels; sustained by sharing bread in food kitchens rather than refectories; sung in spirituals and blues rather than Bach chorales; celebrated in borrowed clothing rather than in eucharistic vestments; growing out of experiences that gradually become the stuff of theological reflection rather than the other way around [*Theology in a New Key*, pp. 24–25].

The Lives of Children

That new situation puts some heavy demands on the rest of us, for those perspectives—to indulge in massive understatement—have not been our perspectives. Two friends, a Protestant and a Jew, have stated the terms of response, encapsulating all oppressions under one. Here is an iconoclastic fellow Presbyterian, John Fry:

> I propose that theologians write theology from the standpoint of the mother in Bombay (or Pittsburgh) whose child has just starved to death. She would not be theology's primary reader, and her situation would not provide theology's subject matter. [But] her rage and grief would provide its angle of vision [*The Great Apostolic Blunder Machine* (Harper & Row, 1978), pp. 174–175].

Alongside that is Rabbi Irving Greenberg, writing after the Holocaust, in which 6 million Jews (including 1.5 million children) died in the crematoria of eastern Europe, and offering a new "working principle" for the future: "No statement, theological or otherwise, should be made that would not be credible in the presence of burning children" (in *Auschwitz: Beginning of a New Era?*, edited by Eva Fleischner [Ktav, 1977], p. 23).

Both Fry and Greenberg make the fate of children a starting point for theological reflection. I propose to accept their converging testimony as defining the moral criterion for any future theology I do: *it must be a theology that puts the welfare of children above the niceties of metaphysics.* Any theology that provides for the creative growth of children will make it satisfactorily on all other scores. Friends in beleaguered Latin America have a vision for the future: "Y los únicos privilegiados serán los niños" ("And the only privileged ones will be the children"). A fit description of the Kingdom of God.

This means that the problems of faith for me today are no longer so much *academic* (the mind/body problem, the relationship of freedom and necessity, the anomaly of God's existence in the world of modern science, the relationship of prayer and autosuggestion) as they are *human-social* (Why does faith not empower people to change? How can we contain the forces of evil? Where is love in a world of burning or starving children? Why are we so reluctant to side with the poor?). *Query:* Are the latter questions "ethical" or "theological"? *Response:* Our shrinking globe has fuzzed the line between ethics and theology. *Query :* Am I a "theological ethicist" or an "ethical theologian"? *Response:* That is the number one nonquestion on my personal agenda.

But theology in a new key not only will reflect on what is going on; it will do so in the light of a history of Christian reflection and experience. The signpost of that heritage has been Scripture. But there is a problem. Scripture has frequently laid a baleful hand on fresh movements of the Spirit, stifling them with sanctions drawn from an era long past. Even so, a "rereading" of Scripture is going on in our day, particularly in situations of oppression, out of which the biblical message is reinforcing the need for change, rather than sanctioning ongoing repression.

The Bible was originally a revolutionary book ("good news to the *poor...*"). We tamed it. Now our sisters and brothers in the Third World are freeing it up once again to communicate its liberating message.

We used to take account of how the Bible was read (by the critics) in Tübingen or Marburg. Now we must take account of how the Bible is read (by the practitioners) in Solentiname or Soweto.

Two different Bibles emerge, depending on the perspective from which the one Bible is read. One perspective very skillfully justifies Western bourgeois capitalist culture. That is the comforting Bible we have read. The other challenges all the assumptions of that culture and offers the ingredients for creating an alternative world, with something about the Kingdom of God being like a little child ("and the only privileged ones will be the children").

Redefining the Task

So, out of reflection on what is going on in a world of injustice, my own theological task has been redefined. Three points of special emphasis are emerging, each enriching and informing the others. One is geographical, a second is historical and cultural, a third is methodological. Here is that agenda, set out with telegraphic brevity:

1. The geographical ingredient I have to take with utmost seriousness is the power of *the voices of the Third World*. Latin America has been my special point of listening, but similar voices are being raised in Asia and Africa. Indeed, to be open to "the voices of the Third World" means to be open to the outcry of those near at hand in the United States as well, to *all* who are dispossessed and exploited, wherever they are, whether for racist, sexist or cultural reasons. Theologies that fail to hear the cries of the hurting, or fail in their responses to seek to overcome the need for those cries, are no longer theologies worthy of attention.

2. The historical-cultural ingredient to which I want to respond is *post-Holocaust Judaism*. Christians, of course, need to listen to Judaism as a

whole, since our historical record vis-à-vis Judaism is worse than our record vis-à-vis any other faith—a devastating indictment. We have killed, tortured, manipulated, proselytized and discriminated against Jews in ways and to a degree that are the shame of our history. But all of this is brought to pinpoint focus in the event of the Holocaust, and what Christians do about it in a post-Holocaust era. The deliberate murder of 6 million Jews, by those who were shaped by an ostensibly Christian culture, makes forever impossible some of our previous theological assertions about (a) the inherent goodness of human nature, (b) a universe in which all things work together for good, (c) any equations between justice and virtue, or (d) just about anything else. A pall is forever cast over complacent or triumphant orthodoxies. There is little of past Christian theology, let us face it, that is "credible in the presence of burning children."

3. For me, the methodological ingredient of this endeavor is *story*. In claiming this I seek not to embrace a "fad" but to recover a lost emphasis. Our faith, after all, did not initially come to us as "theology," and particularly not as "systematic theology." It came as story. Tell me about God: "Well, once upon a time there was a garden . . ." Tell me about Jesus: "Once upon a time there was a boy in a little town in Palestine called Nazareth . . ." Tell me about salvation: "Well, when that same boy grew up, he loved people so much that the rulers began to get frightened of him, and do you know what they did? . . ." Tell me about the church: "Well, there were a great many people who were attracted to Jesus and started working together: Mary and Priscilla and Catherine of Siena and Martin Luther and Martin Luther King and John (several Johns: John Calvin, John Knox, John XXIII) and Gustavo and Mother Teresa, and do you know what they did? . . ."

Out of such stories the systems begin to grow, with results we know only too well: stories about a garden become cosmological arguments; stories about Jesus become treatises on the two natures; stories about salvation become substitutionary doctrines of atonement; stories about the church become by-laws of male-dominated hierarchies. Who could care less?

In losing the story we have lost both the power and the glory. We have committed the unpardonable sin of transforming exciting stories into dull systems. We have spawned system after system: Augustinian, Anselmian, Thomistic, Calvinistic, Lutheran, Reformed, orthodox, liberal, neo-orthodox, neo-liberal. Historically they were very different; today they share in common an inability to grab us where we are and say, "Listen! This is important!"

Retelling the Christian Story

We must *recover the story* if we are to recover a faith for our day. Each of us has his or her story. Alongside them is the Christian story, a story of the heroes and heroines of faith. Could the pair of stories impact one another? Sometimes we hear another person's story and we say, "Aha! that's *my* story too. In hearing about Abraham Lincoln or Jane Addams or Billie Jean King or Coretta King, I am learning about myself." Our theological task is to find ways to "tell the old, old story" so that the listener says, "Aha! That's *my* story too. In hearing about Abraham or Sarah or Jeremiah or Judas I am learning about myself."

The three approaches are interrelated. Story is the interrelating factor. Third World Christians reflect on their situation of oppression and the need for liberation; they reread the biblical story of people-under-oppression-who-are-being-liberated, and find their present story being informed and guided by the ancient one. The Exodus story becomes their story. A similar thing has happened among post-Holocaust Jews, attempting to recover a sense of identity after all identity has been stripped away. Elie Wiesel's writings have become for me a galvanizing example. In a series of novels he explores what it means to be a Jew living in a world in which Auschwitz could take place. The stories at first are very contemporary. But soon the 18th and 19th century Hasidic tales begin to be woven in. Then earlier midrashic commentary on Scripture makes its appearance. Recently he has been retelling tales from the Hebrew Scriptures. None of this is an evasion of the present. It is an attempt *to understand the present by making use of the past.* In retelling the ancient tales, Wiesel informs us, he comes to understand who he is today. The old story becomes his story.

Both Third World theologians and post-Holocaust Jews have been recovering stories from the past that help them understand their own stories in the present. The convergence is too marked to be capricious. It suggests the appropriate theological task for Christians in the future: to explore the ways that stories are told, all kinds of stories, to see if that could help us uncover a way of retelling the Christian story so that listeners, confronted by such retelling, could say, "Aha! That's my story too."

Once we have done that, there will be plenty of time to worry about systems.

Fragments of a Credo

Let me conclude on the personal level after all, since I am afraid that many of us use expositions of What We Think in order to hide Who We Are.

Fragments of a credo:

I believe that the ultimate disposition of who or what I am (death is closer than it was a decade ago) is in the hands of Another, and that those hands are ultimately sustaining and gracious, however sternly they may have to deal along the way with such recalcitrant cargo as I.

I believe that I get clues enough and to spare about the nature of reality not only from ongoing confrontation with the Jesus story but even from occasional confrontation (usually through another person) with Jesus himself.

I believe that such clues are confirmed a hundredfold by who my wife is, who my children are, and who a few incredibly dear friends continue to be.

I believe that I am part of a further circle, beyond those just named, who occasionally manage to put others ahead of themselves, and God ahead of all (no contradiction there), a circle to which in my more affirming moments I give the name of "church."

I believe that there are tasks to do that give meaning to our lives, and that the degree of our own individual success or failure is of little consequence, since God empowers others to pick up and fulfill whatever we do for good, and to transform and redeem whatever we do for ill.

I believe that conversion is not only about changing individual hearts but also about changing social structures, not just cosmetically but radically. This means chipping away at, and perhaps destroying, many things we have taken for granted (for granite), and building into our own situation what many Third World friends have found to be true in theirs, that "to know God is to do justice."

I believe there are little moments during which vast things happen: when bread is shared in certain ways; when brisk walks in the woods are shared with certain persons (sheer gift: an entire fall of this in 1979); when someone else says "thank you" to me, or when I remember to say "thank you" to someone else; when children rise up and bless us simply by who they are; when Beethoven string quartets (recently rediscovered after some fallow years) pierce us with both the joy and the woe of our being, the same joy and woe that William Blake assured us were "woven fine, a clothing for the soul divine."

I believe that our lives provide the occasion for flashes of fulfillment, no matter how much they are threatened by surrounding darkness; indeed, we can begin to deal with surrounding darkness, because we have it on high authority that light shines in the darkness and the darkness has not overcome it.

Beautiful ending. Crescendo or diminuendo (take your choice) to a compelling biblical image . . .

Poignancy and Anger

But, as much as I'd like to, I really can't stop there. I must also attest to a further reality. Let me call it by two names—poignancy and anger. Poignancy, on a personal level, that the sense of the reality of the arms of the Other is sometimes very distant, and poignancy also that many of the things close at hand are fragile: a lot of those books won't get written, some of those friends are all but out of reach, family ties are tested more and more by instances (both in time and space) of separation, challenging tasks often seem overwhelming, and sometimes even Beethoven (and attendant witnesses) are more reminders of the pain of the unattainable than they are the benediction of the achieved.

But more than poignancy (which can be self-indulgent) there is anger—anger not about my own situation so much as about the situation of so many others. Anger that the world is such that fulfilled lives are denied to most, especially to children. Anger at systems that macerate and lacerate their victims, whether the systems are called capitalism or education or fascism or church bureaucracy. Anger at insensitivity on the part of those (myself included) who have it made under any of those systems or combination thereof, and fail to realize that their (our) well-being is purchased at the cost of destruction to so many others. Anger that it is not possible to use the word "socialism" and still communicate with most of the people with whom I want to communicate. Anger at those who from positions of ease scorn liberation theology as "naïve" or "violence-prone" or "reductionist." Anger at God—yes—for so many gaping silences between the fleeting embodiments of the Word we so desperately need to hear and see. Anger at people who attack gays or blacks or women or Jews or Hispanics (or whoever is next on the social hit list) with a loveless spite or lofty superiority that leaves me frightened at my inability to frame responses that are not replications of all that I abhor in them.

Not such a beautiful ending. But at least a more honest one.

"Be ye angry, and sin not," Paul admonishes us. I embraced the first three words of that injunction pretty efficiently in the '70s. Maybe the biggest change I need in the '80s is the gift of being embraced by the last three as well.

Contributors

Peter L. Berger is professor of sociology at Boston College and author of *Pyramids of Sacrifice*, *The Heretical Imperative* and *Facing up to Modernity: Excursions in Society, Politics, Religion*.

José Míguez-Bonino is a theological educator from Argentina and author of *Doing Theology in a Revolutionary Situation* and *Room to Be People: An Interpretation of the Message of the Bible for Today's World*. He is also active as one of the vice-presidents of the Permanent Assembly for Human Rights in Argentina.

Robert McAfee Brown is professor of theology and ethics at Pacific School of Religion, Berkeley, and author of *Theology in a New Key: Responding to Liberation Themes* and *Creative Dislocation–The Movement of Grace*.

Frederick Buechner is a Presbyterian minister and writer, whose latest book is *Godric*. His other novels include *Lion Country*, *The Final Beast*, *Open Heart* and *Love Feast*.

John B. Cobb, Jr., is Ingraham Professor of Theology at the School of Theology at Claremont and author of *The Structure of Christian Existence*, *Christ in a Pluralistic Age* and *Christian Natural Theology Based on the Thought of Alfred North Whitehead*.

James H. Cone is Charles A. Briggs Professor of Systematic Theology at Union Theological Seminary, New York, and author of *God of the Oppressed* and (with Gayraud S. Wilmore) *Black Theology: A Documentary History, 1966–1979*.

Harvey Cox is professor of theology at Harvard University Divinity School and author of *The Secular City*, *The Feast of Fools*, *The Seduction of the Spirit* and *Turning East*.

Langdon Gilkey is Shailer Matthews Professor of Theology at the Divinity School, the University of Chicago, and author of *Reaping the Worldwind*, *Message and Existence* and *Society and the Sacred: Toward a Theology of Society in Decline*.

James M. Gustafson is University Professor of Theological Ethics at the University of Chicago and author of *Protestant and Roman Catholic Ethics: Perspectives for Rapprochement* and *Ethics in a Theological Perspective*.

Carl F. H. Henry, who was founding editor of *Christianity Today* (1956–68), is lecturer at large for World Vision International and author of the multivolume *God, Revelation and Authority*.

John Hick is professor of theology at Birmingham University and Danforth Professor of Religion at Claremont Graduate School. He is the author of *Death and Eternal Life* and *Christianity and Other Religions*.

Martin E. Marty is associate editor of *The Christian Century* and Fairfax M. Cone Distinguished Service Professor at the Divinity School, the University of Chicago. He is the author of *Righteous Empire, A Nation of Behavers, By Way of Response* and *The Public Church: Mainline–Evangelical–Catholic*.

John Mbiti is on the staff of the Ecumenical Institute at Bossey, Switzerland, and author of *African Religions and Philosophy* and *The Prayers of African Religion*.

Jürgen Moltmann, who teaches at the University of Tübingen, West Germany, is author of *The Passion for Life: A Messianic Lifestyle, Experiences of God* and *The Future of Creation*.

Schubert M. Ogden is professor of theology and director of the Graduate Program in Religious Studies at Southern Methodist University, Dallas. His most recent book is *Faith and Freedom: Toward a Theology of Liberation*.

Wolfhart Pannenberg, who teaches theology at the University of Munich, West Germany, is author of *Jesus–God and Man, Theology and the Philosophy of Science, Faith and Reality* and *Human Nature, Election and History*.

Rosemary Radford Ruether is Georgia Harkness Professor of Applied Theology at Garrett-Evangelical Theological Seminary, Evanston, Illinois, and author of *Religion and Sexism, Faith and Fratricide, New Woman–New Earth, The Radical Kingdom* and *Mary–The Feminine Face of the Church*.

Letty M. Russell is associate professor of theology at Yale Divinity School and author of *Human Liberation in a Feminist Perspective* and *The Future of Partnership*.

Nathan A. Scott, Jr., is Commonwealth Professor of Religious Studies and Professor of English at the University of Virginia. He is the author of *Three American Moralists: Mailer, Bellow and Trilling, The Legacy of Reinhold Niebuhr* and *Mirrors of Man in Existentialism*.

David Tracy is professor of theology at the Divinity School, the University of Chicago, and author of *Blessed Rage for Order: The New Pluralism in Theology* and *The Analogical Imagination: Christian Theology and the Culture of Pluralism*.

Paul M. van Buren is professor of religion at Temple University. He is the author of *The Secular Meaning of the Gospel, The Burden of Freedom: Americans and the God of Israel* and *Discerning the Way: A Theology of the Jewish-Christian Reality.*

Elie Wiesel is the author of such works as *Night, The Jews of Silence, The Gates of the Forest, A Beggar in Jerusalem* and *The Testament.*